T0381174

My Simple Prayers

One Woman's God Stories Initiated by Simple Prayers

Karen Jensen Langsam

WESTBOW
PRESS®
A DIVISION OF THOMAS NELSON
& ZONDERVAN

WestBow Press books may be ordered through booksellers or by contacting:

WestBow Press
A Division of Thomas Nelson & Zondervan
1663 Liberty Drive
Bloomington, IN 47403
www.westbowpress.com
844-714-3454

ISBN: 979-8-3850-2969-3 (sc)
ISBN: 979-8-3850-2970-9 (hc)
ISBN: 979-8-3850-2971-6 (e)

Library of Congress Control Number: 2024914835

Print information available on the last page.

WestBow Press rev. date: 01/09/2025

DEDICATION

I dedicate this book to my husband, Andy. Without you, this book would not have become a reality. Had we chosen to live our lives in a way that did not honor the Lord, our stories would not be the same, and our lives would be significantly different. Honestly, I do not believe we would have stayed together for three plus decades without help from the Lord.

Thank you, sweetheart, for your unconditional love, your forever forgiving heart, your strong leadership, and your complete willingness to go with the flow. Your emotional, financial, and technical support encouraged me to begin and continue this writing ministry. You are a gift from the Lord that keeps on giving.

I look forward to serving the Lord with you for the next three decades. His good and perfect will be done.

I love you.

ACKNOWLEDGEMENT

I am deeply indebted to the multiple friends and family who made time to read this book which the Lord entrusted me to write. Sandy, Barbara, Elizabeth, Joanie, and Verne read my initial draft and provided constructive feedback and encouragement. Later, my husband, Andy, my mother, Joan, and two groups of beloved friends made the time and expended the energy to pilot the book and the All-Inclusive Workbook which includes my life lessons learned from those amazing God stories. Those friends include Angela, Anna, Christine, Dolores, Heather, Gloria, Jenn, Joan, Jo Ann, Kim, Kristina, Latasha, Ruth, Sabine, Sue, Suzi, and Zona. Some of these cherished friends have known me for most of my adult life. One of them has known me since middle school. My other precious friends are my new God-sent friends who have known me for less than two years. To you all, please know that it was your words of encouragement, wisdom, and insight that spurred me on to completion.

Three dear friends took a lot of their time and energy to help bring this book to you. Gloria Riddle, Kim Horst, and Stacy Howdeshell spent countless hours editing the book and workbook. One of our Bible study teachers, Kimberly Williams, took the time to read through both book and workbook to give me suggestions and ensure the workbook was biblically sound. Another dear friend of mine, Patricia Anthony, surprised me with the beautiful color layout of the book. I am blown away by the commitment and love shown by these extraordinary, godly ladies. I am also grateful to two local churches that have gone over and above to help me on this journey of obedience. Pastor Jon Robbins and Stuart for so kindly and hospitably hosting our local pilot group at St. Paul's Church. You both have been a blessing to our local group and me. It's refreshing to be blessed by a church that knows no walls. The other church is Horizon Christian Fellowship in Fort Pierce. I am indebted to the pastor's wife and Bible study teacher, Sandy Hennesey, for inviting me to share information on the book and for allowing me to speak on forgiveness to her beloved Agape Madres Bible Study group. Telling all of you thank you does not seem sufficient. My hope and prayers are that our efforts will bless many others and ultimately change lives all for His glory. The last person to invest his time editing and sharing insight regarding my book and workbook was J.R. Crooks. What a joy it is to see so many people lend a hand to bring this book and workbook to fruition. God is good and faithful!

CONTENTS

AUTHOR &
BOOK INTRODUCTION

Where do I begin? Humbled by the insights I have learned and the miracles I have experienced leading to the writing of this book. I cannot wait to share many of my amazing stories of being led by the Almighty, all sparked by a simple prayer. But before I dig in, I want to give you some background information about me. Here we go.

My name is Karen Jensen Langsam. I am the daughter of a dedicated and gifted chiropractor, Harry W. Jensen, and a brave and adventurous woman, Joan P. Jensen. As I affectionately called them, Joan and Harry were married until death did they part. Before my dad went to be with the Lord, my parents raised six humans. They are all beautiful on the inside and the outside. I have had the privilege of "bringing up the caboose" of those six. Presently, Joan faithfully prays for her ever-growing family, including twenty-one grandchildren and currently eight great-grandchildren with more on the way.

My incredible husband of three decades, Andy, has enjoyed the blessing of raising five amazing children with me. We have three daughters and two sons. The birth order is staggered: girl, boy, girl, boy, girl. A few years after I retired from the business world, the Lord put on my heart to educate our children at home. My mother lovingly helped me teach all five of our children for twelve and a half years. I am not superwoman. Without a lot of additional help over the years, I could not have accomplished what the Lord had put on my heart to do. Currently, our youngest is in a brick-and-mortar school. You will get to know us in the following pages as I share some of my God stories with you. My desire is that you get to know Jesus and fall deeply in love with Him through these stories and biblical truths I have learned along the way. I have no experience as an author, but I have spent a lot of time in His Word and in prayer. These pages are a labor of love and an act of obedience.

I diligently began working on *My Simple Prayers* when God called me to write this book in October of 2013 after recovering from a serious disease. Another serious health trial put this book on the back burner. The second health trial took my eyes off the prize. Thankfully, God is faithful even when we are not. Finally, in offering it to you, I hope to bring Him glory through these astonishing and amazing stories and prayers. Though they happened to me, they are truly His stories. I share them and much more because you never know who will pray for you and encourage you to return to your first love, Jesus. Someone you are praying for right now may be the person God Almighty uses to rebuke you gently. Someone you are praying for right now may be the person Adonai uses to drive you to the hospital. Someone you are praying for right now may become your child's in-loves (in-laws). Someone you are praying for right now may become a mighty man or woman of God serving in ministries across the globe. You never know how full-circle Jehovah may go in answering your prayers for others and later bringing it back as a blessing to you—in a beautiful tapestry of grace.

I pray you will be inspired, as I have, and want to jump right into this amazing journey of life with the best friend you could ever have, the Creator of the universe.

1

LITTLE OL' ME

*"Dear Heavenly Father, come into my life, forgive me of
my sins and be Lord of my life, in Jesus's name. Amen."*

After completing my first year of college in 1985, I took off for the Windy City to intern for IBM, the computer hardware and software giant. My parents helped me fill my car with all my worldly possessions as I prepared to leave our small town. I headed to the suburbs to live and be close to my oldest brother, Tom, for protection. I moved in with one of his female friends who resided on the floor directly below my brother's apartment for the summer.

My roommate was tall and thin, with dark hair and an olive complexion. She sold pharmaceuticals. Sporting her advanced business degree, she was a determined businesswoman. My brother was focused on finishing his degree to become a doctor. Tom had many interesting friends. One was a handsome school buddy who wanted to get to know me better. I could tell it was going to be an exciting summer.

Crew, Tom's friend, was unique, unlike anyone else I had met. For example, he was kind and showed genuine concern to the people working in the tollbooths. Yes, kindness to strangers in the city was an unusual trait. He was funny, gentle-spoken, slow to anger, and a genuinely honest man. He invited me to a Phil Keaggy concert. Phil, a gifted musician, songwriter, and guitarist, is also a proclaimed follower of Christ. Unusual for a musician, Phil played guitar without all his digits. Intrigued by the musician and interested in the man who invited me, I went to the concert. Phil Keaggy shared his testimony during the concert.

After the concert, Crew told me the most exciting but straightforward bit of information that would change my life forever: the Creator of the universe wanted to have a personal relationship with me. Yes, that is correct, little ol' me. How powerful is that good news? How could I refuse? My parents raised me in the church where the pastor and Sunday school teachers taught the Trinity. As part of the catechism, I memorized the Lord's prayer, along with the sixty-six books of the Bible. However, the thought that He, the Creator of the universe, God Almighty, wanted to have a personal relationship with me blew me away! How could this be? Of course, I wanted to have a relationship with Him. I prayed with my friend, *"Dear Heavenly Father, come into my life, forgive me of my sins, and be Lord of my life, in Jesus's name. Amen."*

After that simple prayer, things in me began to change. Crew and I regularly attended Willow Creek Community Church, not just on the weekends but also during the extra services during the week. I could not get enough of the rich biblical teaching. My life had changed; I had changed. I became a new creation in Christ.

2

HEARTBREAKING DISOBEDIENCE

"Lord, if it is Your will, bless our relationship.
If it is not Your will, break it off. Amen."

My sophomore year was quickly approaching, and the forty-hour-a-week summer internship was winding down just in time for me to head back to school. However, IBM was not done with me yet. They asked me to transfer to a school in the Windy City to continue working for them while completing my undergraduate degree. Excitedly, I agreed. I could stay close to my new boyfriend and enjoy making some money. Being a broke college student is never fun. Unfortunately, I missed the deadline for attending Northwestern University as a regular student, but their night school was the next best option for me. With IBM behind me, it was a no-brainer.

My relationship with Crew became serious quickly. "Could he be the *one*?" I asked myself. One long weekend in the crisp fall air, he flew home to tell his parents all about me. He was six years older than me, and he wanted to settle down after completing his doctorate at the National College of Chiropractic. While he was on his trip, I shared a concern with an older and more mature couple in the Lord. It was regarding healthy boundaries while dating. Much to my surprise, but welcomed, they laid hands on me and prayed for me to receive the Holy Spirit. It happened powerfully! I remember beginning to pray in a way that was so foreign to me, yet it felt so natural. Again, something strange but so extraordinary happened during that prayer. They suggested I pray and ask for God's will regarding my relationship.

Of course, God would want me to be with the man who led me to the Lord, right? I prayed boldly, completely expecting that to be the outcome. I was totally trusting for His will to be done. My simple prayer went something like this: *"Lord, if it is Your will, bless our relationship. If it is not Your will, break it off. Amen."*

My friend returned. Crew called and said he had news for me and wanted to talk. I knew before he spoke, the Lord had answered my simple prayer. The older, wiser couple who prayed for me in the suburbs of Chicago had their prayers answered powerfully. I guess I did too.

My boyfriend said he was so excited about our relationship that he had told his parents all about me and that he had wanted to propose marriage on his return. However, everything changed on the flight home. I will never forget those words. "Karen, it was the strangest thing. While in flight, I felt the Lord lay on my heart to break off our relationship." Crew paused and then continued sharing, "I do not understand why." He did not understand why, but I did. My gut felt like it had received a firm punch without restraint. He was thirty thousand feet in the air when we were praying. God answered my prayer all right, just not how I wanted.

Sin has its consequences, and I was suffering because of it. We both suffered for it. I loved him. Heartbroken, I, too, thought we were to marry. How could this happen? How could the Lord use this person to lead me to accept Him and then take that person away? I cried out, *"Why, Lord, why?"* I heard nothing. The lack of response was my answer. Deep down inside, I knew our relationship was not honoring Him. I had broken God's heart. I struggled. Here I was the one who had sinned against God, but I was the one angry at Him for the consequence I rightly suffered. Never in my life had I been furious at God. The livid feelings I had toward Him were extremely foreign to me.

3

THE WORD BRINGS BLESSINGS

"Lord, I gave all I had. Now I can't pay the tolls to get home. Please help if it is Your good and perfect will."

Brokenhearted and newly single, I needed to find a new church to call home. The good news was that even though I was struggling, I stayed in the Word by attending a church in the Chicagoland area. Giving into my curiosity, I drove my Volkswagen Beetle to the church that I had heard so much about from friends. It had a reputation as being a "holy roller" church. Sure enough, people of all ethnicities and socioeconomic backgrounds gathered in that place to worship God Almighty. It was a unique experience and a powerful time of worship. I did not know the lyrics or the tunes, but that did not matter. The Lord put it on my heart to give all I had the first time I attended as they passed the offering baskets. Even though the fifty dollars in my wallet was supposed to last me the week, I gave it so effortlessly.

God was so sweet. Approaching the manual tollbooth on my way home, I quickly realized I had no cash. I assumed the tollbooth person would give me an envelope with the toll charge for me to pay for it later. Then it hit me; I have a big God. Why not ask for what I need? My simple prayer went something like this: *"Lord, I gave all I had. Now I can't pay the tolls to get home. Please help if it is Your good and perfect will."* The result of my simple act of obedience showed me that God, the Creator of the universe, had my back. On the way home, random drivers in front of me paid for *all* my tolls. What I experienced does not typically happen. Multiple drivers in different cars must have heard from the Lord and then paid my toll.

The charismatic church in Chicagoland is where I stepped out in faith, took the plunge, and was baptized as a believer. Remembering the announcement of the upcoming baptism at the local YMCA, I returned in my VW Bug unaccompanied. Many strangers surrounded me; however, I was not alone. The sweet presence of the Holy Spirit was with me as a pastor carefully immersed me in the chilly chlorine-filled pool. If the Lord did not wash away the sin, the chlorine did—any germs in the water were dead too! The old self had passed away, and the new had come!

—

During my internship, I noticed the new hires at IBM were from Ivy League institutions. I decided the city was not the place for me—not yet. Full-time education was what I needed. Rethinking my future, I moved home. I said goodbye to Chi-town, Northwestern, and IBM. Next, I said hello to my hometown and community college.

While living in my parents' home during my six-month stay, I overheard a conversation between my father and my brother Bill, who is closest to me in age. My brother inquired, "What has happened to Karen?" Bill had noticed a dramatic change in me for the better. I remember my dad's response, which hurt me: "It is just a phase she is going through." You see, I had changed from the inside out. My dad saw it. My brother saw it. My entire family noticed. I guess they did not like the kinder, gentler Karen. Unfortunately, the pull of the world and the lack of solid biblical teaching were too strong for this new believer. In time, even though I was filled with the Holy Spirit, it was easier to be casual about my faith and ignore God than pursue a relationship with Him. It brings me considerable grief to admit that I returned to many of my old ways.

4

NEW BEGINNINGS

"Lord, should I keep working?"

T wo and a half years passed by quickly from the time I left Chicago and returned to the city with my Finance degree in hand. The day after graduation from Northern Illinois University, I packed up and moved back to the city. This time, at twenty-one years old, I moved into a tiny studio apartment in

Lincoln Park. A day later, I started my career at First National Bank of Chicago. I enjoyed learning about the banking and financial industry firsthand rather than spending time in the classroom. Auditing was not my cup of tea, but it did provide a good salary. A year and a half later, I landed my dream job at IBM with much persistence and great connections from my internship. While working for this company I met the love of my life, Andrew. I married him at the age of twenty-four. I ditched my middle name for my maiden name and became Karen Jensen Langsam.

Andy and I met while we were both newbies at IBM. He lived in Houston, Texas, while I lived in Chicago, Illinois. Unfortunately, this intriguing man was geographically undesirable! After Andy had finished his twelve months of sales training, he attended an invitation-only class to the prestigious Watson Research Lab in Yorktown Heights, New York. I had completed six of the twelve months of the sales training. Before being thrust early into my new territory, my branch manager, Kenny, invited me to attend one last educational class. Little did I know that my future husband would be there too.

In preparing to catch a flight to the Big Apple, my best friend, Eunice, asked me what I would do if I met and became interested in another IBM man. Days before departing, I had broken off a relationship with a fellow IBMer who wanted to marry me and move me to Minnesota. But he was not a faithful man. I quickly exclaimed with much conviction, "I have no desire to date another IBMer ever again!" Eunice, a brilliant, kind, thoughtful, and beautiful young woman who worked as a Systems Engineer at IBM and understood the impending class dynamics.

Eunice had hit the proverbial nail on the head. The invitation-only class contained well educated, good-looking men and a handful of beautiful, intelligent women. During the first session, I took note of a young man in the back. He was asking intellectual questions and dialoguing with these brilliant scientists. However, when he stood, I noticed his height. I preferred the tall, dark, and handsome type. He was dark and handsome, but he missed the mark on height! Taking note of his less-than-tall stature, my interest in him plummeted. However, he proceeded to sign up for all the breakout sessions that I had signed up to attend during the next couple of days. Turning toward him, I calmly and curiously asked, "Are you purposely signing up for the same sessions?" He immediately answered, "Yes, do you mind?" With much poise and purpose, I responded, "No, I do not mind." I proceeded with an invitation. "Would you join my friends and me for lunch?" My response blew me away. Did I not just tell my best friend a few days ago that I wanted nothing to do with another IBMer? The flame was ignited between us.

The romance birthed at Watson Research Lab in 1991 resulted in a commitment to marry one year later. Kind negotiations began between our branch managers. After introducing me to the Texas culture, Andy hit a homerun with a night out enjoying country music and the chicken dance. However, I did my best to persuade Andy to move to Chicago. Somehow, the Cubbies and summer fun in Lincoln Park did not cut it. After he showed me the prices of houses in the Houston area, I chose to move. My branch manager, Michelle, reluctantly approved the transfer from Chicago to Houston.

At my first branch meeting in Houston, Andy wanted to introduce me to one of his friends. He grabbed my arm and said, "Karen, I'd like you to meet my friend Kim." Both of our faces lit up. "Kim, the cheerleader?" I excitedly announced. "Karen, my biology partner?" She returned the positive energy. We hugged and could not believe after all those years we were together again. We reminisced about our mutual friends and stories from Augustana College in Rock Island, Illinois.

Our short-lived college friendship in the Quad Cities was now in full swing. We bought houses in the same neighborhood. We exercised together. I was the second baseman, and she was the third baseman on our coed IBM-sponsored softball team. I am sure she was not happy when I left IBM to work for BMC Software. At least we were still living in the Houston area. We remained good friends and enjoyed serving together on the board of the Greatwood Women's Club. We played bunco and an easy version of bridge. We had a great group of friends who were beginning to grow their little families. The blessing of being reunited with an old friend made the move from Chicago to Houston smooth. And that brings me to the next incredible God story.

—

The year was 1997. While putting our only child, Christiana, to bed, I fell into a deep sleep in her "big-girl" bed. A dream danced in my head. It was wild and vivid. My body took flight while praising the Lord with all my heart, mind, soul, and strength. Never had I praised Him like that. In my dream, my feet were off the ground, and my hands were lifted high in the air. The only thing that contained me in our daughter's bedroom was the bright white popcorn ceiling and the four pale-yellow walls with Winnie the Pooh wallpaper border.

I noticed a small family with their feet on the ground: a man, his wife, and two small children. In front of them shone a brilliant, beautiful light radiating from the small opening on a wooden cased door. The opening resembled a keyhole. Intuitively, I knew my job was to lead this small family to put their hand over the keyhole to receive the brilliant light. Their job was to trust the light.

Awakened from my dream, I was surprised by the creativity of my obviously overactive brain. I prayed. My simple prayer was five sincere words. *"Lord, should I keep working?"* Do not ask me why I asked this question. It simply came to my forethought. It did not make sense to ask that question. At that time in my life, I was a successful businesswoman selling software for a Fortune 500 company making a six-figure annual income. Life was good. Our baby girl was cared for during the day by a lovely young woman named Esmerelda. She adored Christiana. We would come home from work to a hot and tasty homemade dinner, a clean house, and our clothes folded and put away. What more could a young professional want? If I saw something I desired, I could buy it. At twenty-nine years old, the world was mine!

My simple prayer, *"Lord, should I keep working?"* is all I asked. Immediately, I received the answer with a single word repeated multiple times. The answer did not come from my head but from an audible voice that spoke sternly to me. As the Lord answered my simple prayer, His words had astounding clarity, strength, and authority. I heard, **"No! No! No!"** The voice sounded as a father speaking to his child in a disapproving, stern, and protective tone. To say I was shocked and thoroughly rattled after hearing Him repeat this two-letter word to me would be putting it lightly.

Ever heard the saying, "The fear of the Lord is the beginning of knowledge?" It is Proverbs 1:7, and it finishes, "but fools despise wisdom and instruction." One second after I heard God Almighty's voice, I took note of a second voice, this time gentler and in my head. It, too, was clear, filled with love. The second voice was like a concerned father trying to warn his beloved child of imminent danger. He said, **"If you don't (resign), something bad is going to happen."** Hearing the first audible voice followed by the second voice solidified the fear of the Lord in me. *What was to happen?* I thought to myself. Without a shadow of a doubt, I knew I needed to quit my job immediately!

I burst into tears as I ran into our bedroom to awaken my husband. My mission was to break the news to him that I had to quit my lucrative career right away. He was startled from his deep sleep. Due to my tears and emotional state, my hubby was worried that something horrible had happened to our little angel. I reassured him that she was perfectly fine and fast asleep. After taking a deep breath, I blurted out, "I have to resign!" I told him in great detail with much emotion about the wild and vivid dream, the resounding audible voice, and the second gentle voice with an ominous warning. He was tired after a long stressful week. Andy assured me everything would be okay, and we would talk in the morning's light.

Before dawn cracked, I pondered how to break this unbelievable, surprising, and shocking news to my boss. Before my hubby's feet touched the ground, I had called my boss, Bill Pitts, the VP of Sales, and let him know that I needed to talk to him as soon as possible. Early Saturday morning is not the best time to call one's boss. He reluctantly agreed to meet later in the afternoon after he finished watching the college football games. It was a very long day's wait.

The wait was over. Bill was available. But I still hadn't answered my own question: how do I tell my manager that I heard the voice of God Almighty, and that it's the reason I am resigning? Retirement sounded better. But the truth is always the best answer when at a loss for a seemingly reasonable explanation.

I did it! At the risk of sounding like a lunatic, I embarked on telling Bill the truth precisely as it had happened. He knew me. Of course, he would not think I was being irrational. Or would he? Before I successfully told him the entire reason why I was resigning, he interrupted me with a fundamental question, "Where are you going to work?" I reassured him that I was retiring and planned to stay home to raise my baby girl. He did not believe my answer. He inquired a second time, "Who is offering you more money?" Did he not know that I was an upright and honest person? Why would I lie about staying home to raise my little girl? The lightbulb went off in my head, and I knew I had to finish telling him everything that had happened the night before.

Mr. Pitts listened intently, knowing I was in my right mind, but he was not fully understanding how to deal with this unique situation. In general, upper management has a unique opportunity to hear some incredible stories about their employees. I am pretty sure this was a new one for him. Being the seasoned executive he was, Bill made no significant inclination of this story being about the "big fish" that got away. After politely listening to me, we agreed I would help him transition my now seeded Fortune 100 accounts to the sales representative he had recently hired. This process would take more than a few weeks, but not too much longer. Remember what the Lord had said to me? **"If you don't (resign), something bad is going to happen."**

Vice Presidents do not become executives of major companies because they take *no* for an answer, especially in sales departments. The week after I spoke with my boss, word spread quickly around the office that I was resigning. The truth made it to the Executive Vice President (EVP) of Worldwide Sales, Rick Gardner. Rick was another ex-IBM employee, and he was my boss's boss. By the end of the week, they called me into Bill's office. He asked in his unique pitched-yet-calm voice, "What would it take to make you stay?" Again, I reassured him that nothing could change my decision. Steadfast, I could replay the miraculous encounter to a tee, and it would send chills through my entire body as I could hear that resounding word spoken as if it was the very first time. I left the meeting with Bill having the last word, "Talk it over with your husband."

Anxiously, I awaited Andy's return home from work to tell him what my company had requested of me. What a week! We sat on the couch together as I took him through the net of my conversation with Mr. Pitts. Andy responded immediately and confidently, "Simple, Karen. Ask for things you know they cannot do." His suggestion was honey to my ears. We came up with a wish list of five things we were sure they would not accept. Staying true to my word, none of it had to do with money. It was about obedience. I would be able to stay home and raise our sweet, innocent baby. We agreed my list was extremely challenging—if not impossible—for this particular company's Vice President of Distributed Sales to accept.

BMC Software was a centric company with its entire workforce housed in their brand new, massive, and lavish building on Beltway 8 in Houston, Texas. All the account salespeople had their own offices. A gourmet restaurant was open for breakfast for the early risers. The employees packed the casual dining area at lunchtime. BMC also provided exceptional cuisine for customer events. The bottom floor housed a top-of-the-line workout gym with a basketball court and locker rooms. The executive floor housed a huge—even for Texas—salt aquarium tank that overlooked the Houston Skyline. Did I mention the cowhide-lined elevators to take the employees to and from the covered parking lot and their offices? We even had a concierge bank in our building for employees. The building intentionally met the needs of the employees from early in the morning to late in the day, so no one had to leave the building. At that time, working outside of the complex was unheard of in the technology sector. Most technology companies' salespeople were in cubicles. Some, however, were beginning to have a few established salespeople work remotely to keep costs down. But not my company. They wanted to see their employees and keep a pulse on what was happening in the sales representatives' territories.

So, my impossible wish list went like this:

1. Work from home with all the technology to support me. (At that time, that included a laptop, a dedicated computer, a phone line, a fax line, a copier, a fax machine, and a cellular phone. As I stated earlier, this was not common nor accepted at that point in time in our company.)

2. Work four days per week with one paid day off each week.
    (Again, I did not know anyone working only four days per week in my highly competitive company or industry.)

3. ???
    (I cannot remember this one for the life of me. Oops!)

4. Pre-sales technical person dedicated to supporting my sales efforts.

(Typically, I had to share from a pool of about six strong System Engineers, SE's. Sharing resources was not easy because the ratio was not good for us Sales Representatives.)

5. Post-sales technical person dedicated to successful installations.
   (I wanted to make sure my customer installations were successful without me having to take full post-sales ownership.)

Monday came, and I had prepared myself to receive my walking papers. During our serious conversation, I laid out my list of impossible requests to my boss. Keep in mind, working from home was not the norm in the 1990s. Right away, he qualified me, "If I can get these five things you are requesting, you will continue to work for me?" Confidently assuming they would never agree, I said, "Yes." He came back to me and said, "I can commit to one through four, but I need to work on number five." I was not happy. He had already qualified me. I had agreed: only if they could meet all five, I would keep working. My word was my word. I still had hope. Later in the day, my hope began to fade as Bill said he would figure out how to make number five happen. Obviously, the EVP cleared it. Now what was I to do? Feeling committed and convicted is no fun.

I was blown away by my company's desire to keep me, but I knew very well that I was not obeying, at least not immediately. "I will hasten and not delay to obey your commands." (Psalms 119:60). Delayed obedience is disobedience. Now, I had to continue to work. Halfway through the fiscal year, my husband and I decided I had to work until I made my quota. Then, I would have met my financial responsibility to BMC for the year. I reached my sales quota in the next three months with some very focused and diligent work. Delighted with my achievement and prepared to resign, I scheduled a meeting with my new boss, the Director of Distributed Systems.

My new boss was not from the great state of Texas. His vibrate vernacular was a bit offensive to me. Somewhat bossy, he genuinely wanted to fit into the southern culture and be successful. He wanted this so much that he was working on cleaning up his colorful language. As soon as I shared my plans to resign, he humbly begged me to stay and help him reach his national quota. His quota included our entire North American Open Systems team. In hindsight, I was foolish for agreeing to his request. Financially, though, this became a brilliant decision for our family. We used my commission checks to pay off our cars, ensuring we had no debt except for our recently purchased five-bedroom home. Thank goodness we had secured a great deal on this relatively new cosmetic fixer-upper. Remember what the second, gentle voice told me? **"If you don't (resign), something bad is going to happen."** Well, my dear friends, something terrible did happen.

5

DISOBEDIENCE HAS ITS CONSEQUENCES

*"Lord, help me not be a stiff-necked person.
Help me to truly forgive my husband."*

I remember the day very clearly. The year was 1998. The excitement of Valentine's Day had come and gone. I departed for the office with our daughter at home in the competent hands of our loving nanny, Esmerelda. My husband returned home from a business trip that had taken him to Peru. While he was away that week, I hosted a customized briefing for my clients that required a lot of entertaining at our headquarters in Houston. The briefing was a success, and they were catching their flights home before noon. Andy was very excited to see me. So excited that we decided to take a break for a late lunch and rendezvous at home. We both traveled for our jobs, typically a week at a time. Occasionally, Andy would be in Asia for two to three weeks. Peru was a new destination.

The five o'clock bell rang! The busy week was finally over. We laid down exhausted from the week's work and the Lord spoke to me again. This time the Lord said, **"Ask what is wrong."** I used those exact words seconds later as we lay in bed that night. He rolled out of bed, fell to his knees, and broke down into tears. I was dumbfounded. I was not expecting an emotional response. He muttered, "If I tell you, I am afraid you will leave me." Now my mind was spinning. "What are you talking about?" I quickly replied. Now he had my undivided attention.

Andy "verbally vomited" what was weighing so heavily on his mind. Whoa, I had not prepared myself for what he had just told me! His confession came totally out of the blue. Initially, I had no concerns. I only asked the question because of the Lord's prompting. Andy was in a bad panic as though the worst from me was coming. I remember the anger of being betrayed. The thought came crashing through my mind that he could have physically harmed me by coming home and getting intimate with me, as though that act would wash away his sins. My anger burned inside me! I was taken aback, almost in shock. Tears flowed from my eyes as my heart broke in two. How could he have so carelessly thrown everything we had together out the proverbial window? *Man, I hate alcohol,* I thought. He would never have done this given a sober mind. Was this the horrible thing the Lord had forewarned me? **"If you don't (resign), something bad is going to happen."**

Andy was repentant on his knees, asking me to forgive

him. Just as out of the blue as the Lord telling me to ask him what was wrong, He told me to say to Andy, **"I forgive you."** I immediately repeated those exact words, "I forgive you." Those words flowed out of my mouth only out of obedience. I could not bear to see my husband begging me for forgiveness. I needed rest.

The next day came. It was Saturday. I picked up the phone to call a counselor. I needed help. My husband physically would not let me make the call. He put the phone down and begged me not to call for help. He was fearful that the person on the other end would advise me to leave him. Honestly, I did not want him anywhere near our daughter and me. The pain of betrayal was too great. I remember holding our daughter, looking down at our pool and yard from our second-story deck. I thought all of this was for nothing. My job, our house, the pool—none of it mattered. All that mattered was my family. I prayed and prayed and called out to the Lord in so much pain.

Exercise has always been part of my life. It provides a way for me to stay fit and have fun. However, while I was rollerblading on that painful Saturday, the exercise provided me with emotional release and time with my best friend! I donned my blades and took off to be alone with God. I needed to hear from Him. I needed Him to listen to me. I was so overwhelmed during my work out that I had to sit on the curb and let out my pent-up emotions. Tears flowed from my eyes as I tried to catch my breath. I wailed as though my best friend had died. What was I to do now? I was so sorry that I hadn't obey right away. Upon returning home, I opened my Bible and researched every scripture I could find about marriage and divorce. I found that I was biblically allowed to divorce him. I found the reason why God allowed divorce. The scriptures were crystal clear—God allows divorce because we are a stiff-necked people. Stubborn. I did not want to be a stiff-necked person. I did not want to be stubborn.

I knew I needed to do what God had told me to say. I needed to forgive him. Not just to say it, I also needed to mean it. I thought, *But how?* How would I forgive someone who I trusted with everything, and who carelessly, in a drunken stupor, threw it away? I prayed and asked for help, *"Lord, help me not be a stiff-necked person. Help me to truly forgive my husband."*

6

OBEDIENCE HAS ITS REWARDS

"Thank you, Jesus!"

About six weeks later, I woke up with an upset stomach. Feeling a bit off with the urge to toss my cookies, I ran to meet the porcelain goddess. Trust me, I do not worship the commode. However, it made me think, *Hmmm.* I decided to take a quick pregnancy test. Before I could do a double-take, I saw the confirming pink line. Oh, my goodness!

What a surprise! The Lord knew I would obey His most recent words to me to forgive my husband. He blessed us with a seed sown the day of my husband's return from Peru. Yes, I was pregnant with our second child! My joyous prayer was simple, *"Thank you, Jesus!"* I love the words in Psalm 127:3-5a which read, "Children are a heritage from the Lord, offspring a reward from him. Like arrows in the hands of a warrior are children born in one's youth. Blessed is the man whose quiver is full of them." God's words of warning, wisdom, and His blessings were perfectly timed on His heavenly calendar.

—

Spring was in full bloom, and the fiscal year was closing. With new resolve and another valid reason to stay home, I marched in to see my new VP of Sales, Jay Gardner. My director missed his quota by a mere $5,000, but I well overachieved my objective. Mr. Gardner had a different agenda for our meeting. Retirement? Nope! Instead, he offered me a manager's job with stock options and any territory in the United States that my little heart desired. Thanking him for the opportunity and knowing he was a strong believer, I told him the story of hearing God's voice.

I proceeded to tell Jay that I was pregnant with our second child, and I planned to stay home to raise our children. He was happy for me. I was elated! I finally did it—-I obeyed! I resisted the temptation that lay in front of me. I had always wanted to be a manager and stock options just sweetened the deal. I left that meeting and, on the way home, realized something significant. I could no longer hear the resounding voice that I had replayed in my head many times. The Holy Spirit-induced goosebumps that had accompanied that majestic and powerful voice in my head were no longer present on my body. The holy voice was no longer available to be replayed. I had done it! I obeyed! The entire management team knew that my retirement from the working world was imminent, and so did the enemy. The Lord had other plans for me.

7

HIDDEN ANGER

"Lord, please forgive me for having hidden anger."

The church was the place for me. An exhaustive search for a church, which took place from the time we married, had finally come to an end. What helped us narrow our search was a recommendation from my pastor back home who married us. Since Andy accepted Jesus as his Lord and Savior at a Baptist church, and I grew up in the Lutheran church, Pastor Gronbach suggested a middle ground. He suggested we try a Methodist church. I did not know much about the Methodist church, let alone John Wesley, but we took his well-intended suggestion, and off we went. Before our second child was born, we found the church we could both call home: Christ United Methodist Church of Sugar Land, Texas.

Rising early on our toddler's schedule, we loved the eight o'clock morning service. Tears would stream down my face during the service, and my husband would give me a perplexed look, not understanding why. However, I knew why. The sweet conviction of the Holy Spirit was upon me. This overwhelming feeling happened over and over again while sitting in the pews. Sometimes, it was during the worship and other times it was during the message. Week after week, I knew I was not the person the LORD wanted me to be. I was not the person I wanted to be. He was gently changing me from the inside out.

A few days after I had retired from the business world, we stayed after church to participate in a potluck lunch. It was a last-minute decision that landed us smack-dab at the very end of the long line. The thin blond lady in front of us had her hands full with three darling towheaded girls. We began some small talk with her. Judi was her name. My husband talked so highly of me around church members. He proceeded to tell her what a saint I was. Really, it was embarrassing. He had put me on a pedestal. I did not like it. *Or did I?* On that day, Judi became a dear friend. As our lives became more inter-twined, my newfound friend quicky became a beloved sister to me.

Before the conversation ended that day, Judi invited us to participate in a couples' Bible study. I am so grateful we accepted her kind invitation because the study was a godsend! Together, Andy and I grew our tattered relationship from Gary Smalley's study called *Making Love Last Forever*. The day is still firmly planted in my mind when the Lord showed me through this study that I had hidden anger toward my husband from what had happened months earlier. Gary's advice was to confess it with one another and ask for forgiveness. We followed his advice, and much needed healing came from the Lord that day. My request to my husband was to forgive me for my hidden anger. Once it was exposed, the grip ended. He forgave me. We prayed together a simple prayer of forgiveness, *"Lord, please forgive me for having hidden anger."* He, too, prayed. A miracle happened! Our broken hearts mended, and joy ushered into our relationship. With that healing and passing of time, I began to trust my husband again.

8

LA CUCARACHA

*"Lord, help me to do a good job with
this ministry. I have no idea how to do
this; please teach me what to do."*

"God's plan for you is to give you hope and a future, not to harm you." (Jeremiah 29:11) This well-known verse rang true for me. Retired, pregnant, and with a small child in tow, I met with our pastor and let him know I was now available to help in any way they needed me. I joined the welcome team. My job was to smile and welcome the people coming into church for service. What a fun job and one my husband and I could do together! From there, they asked me to run the welcome team. That included scheduling the greetings and coordinating the volunteers to follow up with new guests. We took them homemade bread. If we were lucky enough to catch them home, we asked if they had any questions about our church or our Lord. I enjoyed this job too. I must have done a decent job, as later they asked me to run the entire evangelism team, which included the welcome team.

Prior to me accepting the responsibility, one speaker in our church said, "The word Evangelism is a 'cockroach' word. Whenever people hear it, they run in fear." It did not scare me. The LORD had put a burden on my heart for the lost. I had no idea what to do or how to do it, but I knew the Lord would help me. My simple prayer was this: *"Lord, help me do a good job with this ministry. I have no idea how to do this; please teach me what to do."*

Help is exactly what I received. I proposed to Pastor Tom that I attend the Willow Creek Evangelism Conference. He agreed, and off I went. The presenters were amazing, and each day was jammed packed. One night during the conference, fast asleep in my hotel room, the Lord gave me an amazing vision of thousands upon thousands of tiny bright lights in the sky. Each light represented new believers in Christ, a future of what was to come. What a glorious sight it was! He spoke to me, and I took copious notes. When I awoke the next day, the vision was almost surreal, as though it had never happened. However, I had a notebook full of information regarding all that I had heard and seen. Again, I received a warning from the Lord but this one had a different focus. He said, **"If you don't, their lights will go out."** I knew He was equipping me and giving me an unquenchable passion for the lost. After seeing this vision and hearing those words, I had a refreshed and deepened love for the not-yet-found.

Departing with a plan, thanks to the fantastic, godly

presenters at the conference, the once handful of people at CUMC became a large, effective evangelism team. God is so faithful! He built a team of volunteers that included apologetics, faith sharing, and the tried-and-true welcome team. We even added a 5K fun run with the help our of our *Rebel with a Cause* young adult Sunday school class to reach out to the community. It's magnificent to watch Him work through others.

9

BABY SCARE

"Lord, give us a healthy baby; if not, Your good and perfect will be done."

"Lord, help Chung come to know You."

D octors warned me that this pregnancy was high risk because of my age. Initial tests showed the baby would most likely have a severe birth disorder such as Down Syndrome. Following the doctors' orders, I scheduled the genetic screening appointment. In addition, our obstetrician (OB) strongly recommended amniocentesis. We were scared and chose to move forward with the test after learning that our OB had pioneered the procedure twenty years earlier. Our doctor only had one amniocentesis end in fatality over decades of his practice. Our skilled physician reassured us that this tragedy was very early in the pioneering stages. We prayed and agreed to move forward in his capable hands. Ultimately, we were trusting God.

Waiting three long weeks for the results was difficult. Yet, it gave us time to talk, pray, and decide what we would do given possible challenging scenarios. We prayed fervently for a healthy baby. *"Lord, give us a healthy baby; if not, Your good and perfect will be done."* We decided then and there, no matter what the health of our unborn baby, we were going to take it the way God had intended. The tests came back false positive, which meant our unborn baby would most likely be healthy. He answered our prayers!

After a full-term pregnancy, our first-born son was alive and well! He had all ten toes and ten fingers. He was a beautiful sight for our eyes. During the pregnancy, the book of Luke became my favorite book of the Bible. What better name for our first-born son than Luke? Our pediatrician came to the hospital to meet his newest patient and to check his health. Then, a specialist in circumcisions, a Jewish Rabbi, performed the procedure. When the Rabbi handed Luke to me, the Lord spoke very clearly to me five prophetic words. I made the mistake of sharing that information with others prior to it coming to fruition. Lesson learned. Now, I store those words in my heart.

—

I was hungry for the Word. I could not wait any longer. About a year or so after initially volunteering at our church, I wrote my name down on a clipboard to register for an in-depth Bible study. It was called Discipleship I. I was committed and excited about what was to come! Shortly after that, I met our two fearless leaders and the other eleven women that embarked on this journey. None of us knew each other in the beginning. However, we became quite close after studying 80% of the Bible over the school year. It was in-depth reading of many chapters in the Bible for five days of the week, then reflecting on the sixth day and resting on the seventh. I loved it! I could not wait to share what I had learned each week and to hear from my new friends. It was a joy to learn with others. Reading the Word blew my mind away almost every day. In fact, I discovered new biblical gems each time I delved into this ageless script.

Each day before diving into the Word, I would spend time with the Lord. I had been praying for the Lord to use me to lead someone, anyone, to Him. I asked over and over. Daily, I would ask the Lord to use me in this way. I even wrote out my prayers expressing my sincere desires. Days turned into weeks, and weeks turned into months of praying. Finally, the day came.

A fantastic photoshoot of our first-born child led me to a local frame shop. The clerk, a young Korean man called Chung (not his actual name), very patiently helped me figure out mats, glass, and potential frames. It was an expensive order for our single-income family's budget. I mentioned that I liked his choice of music, which was playing on a compact disc in the store. He offered to burn a copy of it for me. My appreciation was evident, and I wanted to share my music with him as well. I made a bold move, and I offered him some of my Christian music. That simple offer opened the door to some conversations about my faith, convictions, and following Jesus.

I could not wait for my next visit to pick up where we left off and get our framed photos. I left there praying all the way home, thanking the Lord for opening the door. Chung was heavy on my heart. This young man wanted to believe in and follow Jesus. However, Chung was at a crossroads. He had a girlfriend, and their relationship did not honor the Lord. Which way would he choose? I prayed earnestly and daily for him. *"Lord, help Chung come to know You."*

During each visit, I could tell from his questions that he was getting closer and closer to accepting the Lord. Good thing I had lots of photos to frame. We never know how or when God is going to use us. I wish I had the opportunity to pray with Chung to accept Jesus as his Lord and Savior there in that little frame shop. I did not. However, the story does not end there.

10

A NEW YEAR AND NEW ADVENTURES

*"Adonai, if this is not Your good and
perfect will, stop the move!"*

F riday night, the eve of a new year, my husband arrived
home from the office with exciting news to share. His Vice
President at BMC Software had asked him to take on a new
responsibility that included a move! I asked, "Where and when?"
He quickly replied, "Canada and immediately." My next set of

questions went like this, "Is it a promotion? Is it more money? And will they pay for our housing?" The answer was "Yes" to all three questions.

We proceeded to get ready to bring in the new year, 1999, with our dear friends, the Kelleys. As we headed to the party, we both knew we were moving. We were excited and apprehensive about what the future had in store for us. Our friends were excited, too, and very supportive, knowing it was a short-term assignment. We brought in the new year celebrating this decision.

The next day, I woke up in complete horror! How in the world did we decide on something as important as a move without praying about it first! I quickly began to beg God, *"Adonai, if this is not Your good and perfect will, stop the move!"*

It was too late. I remember sitting in church that Sunday morning wondering what was ahead of us. I was worried because we did not seek His will first. Moves were challenging for me. I remembered the last time I left loved ones behind. A few days after our wedding, we left my small town in a tiny Ryder truck with all my worldly possessions. Andy and I crammed into the front cabin. We hadn't even driven ten miles outside of my hometown before we had to stop abruptly. I got out and dry-heaved on the side of that country road. I had not eaten breakfast, it was just the masked pain of leaving my family and my small town behind which had made me sick to my stomach. After that flashback, I thought, *here we go again.*

After the service, we told Pastor Tom that we were moving as quickly as we could find a rental home in Canada. He and Susan, my direct report, would need to arrange for someone to take over my lay leadership position. Reverend Pace mentioned, "Canada is known as a godless country." Upon hearing that news, my heart broke! How could we go there? I prayed more fervently, *"Please, Lord, if this is not Your will, please stop this move!"* It was to no avail—the move proceeded. I decided to have a good attitude. What else could I do? Quickly, we prepared to move. BMC worked with us to schedule a house-hunting trip followed by a moving truck in less than a month. Our entire house was packed up, shipped, and detained across the US-Canadian border. We waited patiently for our belongings. In February, we moved into a furnished short-term rental home in Ontario. In March, we moved into our home away from home.

During that whirlwind month filled with preparations to move, the Lord gave us a plan to take care of our home in Sugar Land while being expatriates. The previous fall, a group of our friends talked us into taking a biblically-based parenting class. They had to work hard to sell us on taking the class since it required an 18-week investment of our time. In addition, both parents had to participate. Since we were all raising our kids together, we agreed it seemed natural to take this class with them. Much to our surprise, we enjoyed it. We learned so much about parenting and how important our marriage was to raise emotionally healthy kids. It was "heart" training. I remember thinking early in the study, *How do you train their hearts?* The mystery was unraveled as it paralleled the other Bible study I was taking at the time. To be capable of training our children's hearts, we had to first train our hearts in the Word. The desire to be pleasing to the Lord is what matters most. It sounds simple now, but it was perplexing at the time. I was like a newborn when it came to reading the Word of God. I had sat through plenty of sermons as a child and had eaten up great messages as a young adult, but daily reading His Word was relatively new to me.

Our parenting class leaders took us under their wings, and we quickly became friends. The wife and I would walk together, as I pushed my two little ones down the streets of their subdivision. We prayed for our husbands, for our children, and for God to be ever-present in our lives. It was a sweet friendship.

I had shared with her that we were moving for a period of one to two years. They, too, were excited for us. The Lord put on my heart to invite their family to rent our home from us. My husband agreed, and we asked them based on the Lord's prompting. She was surprised and excited! Elated, she explained that they had been praying about where to live. Their lease was ending soon, and they would need a new place to call home. It was a done deal. They blessed us by living in our home, helping to cover some of the monthly expenses associated with our property. We were blessing them with a beautiful home, more room to homeschool their children, and a pool to play in. It worked out perfectly. God has the best ideas!

11

WELCOME TO O'CANADA

"Lord, bring who You want to help me manage this home so I may spend more time with my sweet children."

U pon our arrival, we were welcomed by the frigid February air. The owner of our rental home could not move out fast enough for us to move in, so we rented a furnished house for one month. It met our basic needs. However, when we arrived, we had to store all our worldly possessions, minus our road bikes and our warmest clothes. We were so excited to move into our new home and furnish it. On occasion, we would casually drive by to show the kids where we would be living.

The older home was beautiful. Large, chiseled stone lined the outside walls of the original structure. A later addition to the home finished off the L-shaped house. The backyard boasted an enormous lap pool with a diving board and a lovely two-story "treehouse" without the tree. We had found the perfect backyard for our young, growing family. Much to our surprise, a green shuffleboard court appeared near the basketball hoop once the snow melted away. For Canada, the home could have been considered a mansion. On more than one occasion, trades or salespeople would knock on the door and ask me, "Is your mother home?" They were expecting a wealthy older Canadian woman, not a youthful American.

This enormous place was too large for me to keep up on my own. So, I prayed, *"Lord, bring whom You want to help me manage this home so I may spend more time with my sweet children."* We quickly took out an advertisement in the local paper and began the search to hire honest help. Ring, ring! Ring, ring! The phone did not stop ringing! The phone interviews helped to cut the candidate list down quickly. Looking for reasons not to hire someone, helped me weed out many potential candidates. One person stood out because of her candidness. After having a lovely chat over the phone, she called me back. Her reason was to make sure I knew her ethnicity. This forthright wife and mother commented, "I am Chinese, and if that is a problem, I understand." My quick and gut response was, "I am American, and if that is a problem, I understand." We both laughed. I knew right then—she was the one. I liked her honesty, her directness from the get-go. Jeni was the name I was to call her.

The name Jeni means a lot to me now: faithful, punctual, caring, trustworthy, and hardworking. She was a lovely lady to have in my home. My new employee's responsibility was to clean and help me around the house from 9-2, Tuesdays and Thursdays, so I could focus on my children. She did everything I asked her to do without complaining. She quickly got into a routine that served my family very well. As I began to get to know this mother of one, I began to trust her more and allowed her to enjoy my kids, Christiana, and Luke. Trusting her with our two children allowed me to take an hour each morning and study God's Word in depth. Little did I know that she was very curious about what I was so enthralled with every morning.

Once she arrived, my routine was to head to the sunroom, sit on the cold slate floor, and read His Word while taking notes. My new hire was watching and observing me. I did not keep what I was doing a secret. When Jeni asked what I was studying, I was happy to share it. I told her, "I am finishing a Bible study that I started at the beginning of the school year in the United States at my old church. It's called Discipleship I. When I complete the study, I will have read close to 80% of the Bible in chronological order." The evangelist in me wanted Jeni to be as excited as I was to learn the Word. I also knew the Chinese people were typically Buddhists. However, that did not stop me from sharing. Jeni became more than my employee. She became a friend. Given all that I was to go through while living in Canada, the Lord knew I needed more than one true friend. I had been praying for good, godly friends in the country I was to call home.

12
MINISTRY BIRTHED

"Lord, bring a strong believer into my life."
"Lord, should we birth
Discipleship Bible Study at our new church?

The Lord answered another prayer of mine. Before moving, I began praying, *"Lord, please bring a strong believer into my life."* He did just that! While touring our soon-to-be school, the principal introduced me to a warm and welcoming Dutch Canadian. She said, "Welcome to Canada! I am Heather." Our friendship began at John Knox Christian School when our four-year-old daughter and I toured that campus. Heather is blonde and beautiful inside and out. Her accent was endearing and the best part about her was her love for the Lord. I knew I would learn much from her. I remember her telling me to always check scripture to make sure that what is said to be the Word was truly written in the Bible. That tip was great advice!

Heather invited us to her church, The Meeting House. Thanks to her invite, we went and found it to be very upbeat—almost edgy—when it came to the interlude music. The alternative music was an initial concern for my hubby. However, the teaching was out of this world! During the sermons, I could not take notes fast enough. I was learning and growing at an exceptional rate with the robust teaching of the Word from the Word. They also had these unique groups called home churches. It was where several would gather once a week to dive deeper into the teaching from the weekend services. I joined a group of other homemakers to review and discuss the teaching. It quickly became one of my favorite things to do during the week. The Meeting House was a great church for our young family, and I had a fantastic experience in the homemakers home church. Both gatherings will always have a special place in my heart.

After sharing information with Heather about the fantastic Discipleship Bible Study I was completing from my old church, she wanted to know more about it. My sweet friend borrowed my study guide and quickly fell in love with the format. We both knew this would help many new and young believers to grow deeper in love with our Lord. The goal was to put "feet on their faith." Heather wanted me to help her birth the Bible study at our new church. Elation is the best word to describe my feelings as she embraced this study as her own. I prayed, *"Lord, should we birth Discipleship Bible Study at our new church?"*

God brought us together for a purpose. We were now a team, and we headed to our pastors to ask their blessing and permission to birth this new study in the country that was supposed to be godless. With all due respect to our pastor back home, Canada is not godless. On the contrary, God is very much alive and working on His behalf around our entire globe.

The lead teaching pastor, the congregational care pastor, and the elders were on board to launch this study at the beginning of the following school year. Busy does not begin to describe the amount of work necessary to birth this study. First came formal Discipleship training in Chicago. Next came advertising. Since the pilot group was made up of key leaders in the church, as well as people near and dear to my heart, the word spread quickly. The goal was to educate potential leaders for future Discipleship groups.

Fall came and we launched the first Discipleship study at The Meeting House. It was great! Our lead pastor kicked off the thirty-two-week Bible study emphasizing the importance of taking the commitment seriously and completing the study without missing more than two of the thirty-two sessions. Our pastor had set up our group to have a fruitful time studying His Word. The group of fifteen included:

- Our congregational care pastor
- Two elders
- My husband
- A handful of hungry new believers
- A brand-new Messianic Jew
- One curious apostate

Of course, we all grew close as friends, with the Lord, and with one another. The self-proclaimed apostate could not resist the love from the author, Abba, as she read His love story to her. She was once a former believer who lived outside the faith for more than half her life, and within six to eight weeks of reading His Word, she was back! Praise the Lord. My new friend recommitted her life to Him as her Lord and Savior. God is so good! Want to know her name? I will save that information for another one of my God stories.

13

WARFARE

"Lord, how can I help her?"

While living in Canada, illogical, unexplained things were happening during the middle of the night in the original side of the house. On multiple occasions our two-year-old son, Luke, would wake up with terrifying nightmares. He would repeatedly scream at the top of his lungs, "Get off of me!" Since I am a light sleeper, I ran to his room to calm him down. I asked, "What in the world happened to scare you so much?" He tearfully replied in a tender yet scared voice, "Large insects were all over me, Mommy, and I couldn't get them off!" In addition to the insect terror, our Siberian Husky would act wildly in the middle of the night as though something was after him. I shared these strange happenings and another very odd story with the father of Christiana's classmate while we walked our children into their school. It turned out Mr. Chang had his Master of Divinity with a Counseling specialization. He kindly offered to teach me how to spiritually cleanse our rental home.

Michael Chang, a gentle, soft-spoken man, came to our house and taught me how to pray throughout the home. All was going well as we prayed through each room until we began to pray in Luke's tiny bedroom. I will never forget the feeling and vision I received as we stood a few steps inside that room. The vision was so graphic that I bolted to the bathroom across the hall and began to dry heave. Michael reassured me that it would be okay and that we had to finish praying through the house. I shared with him the vision of what had happened in that bedroom. The memory of it still breaks my heart, and due to the graphic nature, I am choosing not to share that vision. Praise God! With prayer, cleansing and healing are possible, which is precisely what happened. Jesus's bloodshed on the cross some two thousand years earlier cleansed the room. Our little Luke never suffered another night of terror in that tiny hunter-green bedroom.

The primary reason I opened up to Michael was to share an extraordinary story. A unique and almost inexplicable event had transpired while visiting friends in Sugar Land. During that trip, we stayed with our dear friends, the Kelley's. After a sweet time watching our kids play together while we caught up, we said good night, and I went to bed. My routine was to pray for everyone on my mental prayer list, including the ladies from my home church back in Canada. I loved those ladies dearly and prayed for them daily. While praying, one of the ladies the Lord had laid heavy on my heart showed up in a vision. I could see Trudy as she was at that moment, bawling her eyes out, bent over on her knees, and distraught. Seeing Trudy that way brought me great pain. I cried out to the Lord, *"Lord, how can I help her?"*

Immediately, I felt my spirit begin to pull away from my body. It started rising toward my head from my feet, through my legs, and into my chest. My breathing became constricted. Fear gripped me! My thoughts turned from wanting to help my friend to protecting my family. The idea of leaving my husband and the question of who would raise our children raced through my mind. I immediately asked the Lord for my spirit to stop leaving my body. As soon as I asked for it to stop, it ceased, and my spirit moved back to its original position. Perplexed as to what had just happened, I wanted to talk with my friend. However, I decided to leave my friend's dire situation in the competent and loving hands of Jesus.

—

Upon returning to Canada and our home church, I could not wait to ask Trudy, "What happened that caused you so much pain?" I wanted to know if everything was all right given what I had seen in the vision. I asked her how she was doing and if she was better than last week. Trudy wanted to know how I knew she had been upset. She said, "I was all alone, and no one was with me." I shared with her my vision and what I experienced. We were both perplexed as to how I could see her in pain thousands of miles away. Trudy explained that her friend was extremely depressed and seemed manic. She had been praying for her and did not know what else to do to help her. I reassured her the Lord had heard her cries and was there for her friend.

God cares and hears our every cry and sees our tears, especially when weeping for others. Saint Paul said to the believers in Colossae, "For though I am absent from you in the body, I am present with you in spirit and delight to see how disciplined you are and how firm your faith in Christ is." (Colossians 2:5, NIV)

I think what Paul is referring to in this verse is similar to what I experienced. Sometimes, God allows us to be with others in spirit when we pray diligently and fervently for them. As strange as it was, I will never forget that experience and how sweet Jesus was for not pushing me once I became afraid of the unknown.

14

DOUBLE TROUBLE

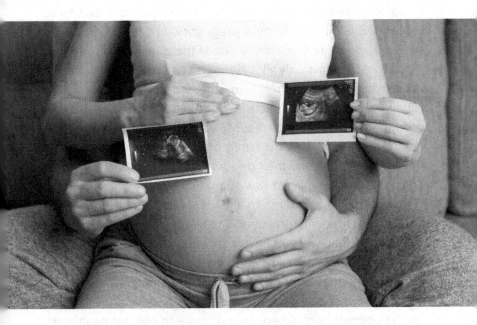

"Lord, why do I feel this way? It's not normal.
Please take this horrible feeling away."

During that intense period of spiritual warfare, while living in our Canadian home, I became pregnant. The thought of another child brought tears of joy to my eyes. Our family was growing, and we could not have been more excited about adding a third child. Remember the five-bedroom fixer-upper that we bought back in Texas? Slowly but surely, we were going to fill it with tiny hands and feet. Then, it hit me: we would have a child with dual citizenship in our family. What an honor and a joy to receive such a blessing!

Of course, our soon-to-be bundle of joy was going to need the best prenatal care. After inquiring to find the most competent doctor for our consideration, we realized Canada's healthcare system was very different from the standard practices of obstetricians in the United States. In the U.S., it is routine to see an OB-GYN to confirm a pregnancy. In Canada, however, seeing a specialist that early is out of the question. A pregnant woman in Canada is only allowed to visit an obstetrician once she has made the 20-week mark. In other words, the unborn baby is half-baked before a specialist is involved. Oh, this realization brought great concern to me. My Canadian friends and one of our pastors assured me the family practitioners have the training to care for women and their unborn children for up to 20 weeks. They reassured me that it was going to be okay.

My friends referred me to a team of family doctors who had been in practice for a long time. The two doctors I saw were very caring, and they were believers. Additionally, my new primary care doctor's office was close to my home. It included a lab in the building, right across the street from the hospital. Andy and I decided this was a good choice for our baby and me. We set up the appointment schedule and chose to use our healthcare insurance and pay the co-pays versus our Canadian visa, which provided full coverage at no charge. It just seemed right for us to pay for the healthcare.

From the first day I knew I was pregnant, I felt very strange. My entire body felt as though it was vibrating, and I was extremely sick to my stomach. I had morning sickness with my other pregnancies, but this one was off the charts. The very low vibration never went away. Every trick in the book did not work. I would feel this strange sensation from the moment I woke up until I fell asleep. Of course, I explained this to my new doctors. They did not know what to make of the vibration sensation. However, the primary doctors believed the sensation would pass with the baby's development. My daily prayer was the following: *"Lord, why do I feel this way? It's not normal. Please take this horrible feeling away."*

The doctors ran the standard tests, including blood work, to ensure everything was in order. I was eager to see the results. So, I called the office in advance of my next visit. The human chorionic gonadotrophin (hCG) is a hormone for the maternal recognition of pregnancy. The hCG level is what I was looking forward to knowing. The lab told me I had to wait until my next visit. Reluctantly, I waited. My doctor conveyed that something had gone wrong, much to his surprise. The tests were grossly inaccurate. I began to wonder and ask myself, "How odd. How is it possible to mess up a simple hCG test?" I asked to see the results. They said they were not available. The healthcare professional I spoke with was not concerned that they were unavailable. I was very concerned! What could have happened to the results? Why were they not available? Were the results so grossly abnormal that they concluded they were invalid? I had too many questions with no answers. It was a very trying first trimester.

—

I remember the night very well. I had been reading a book by C.S. Lewis called *Mere Christianity*. Reclined in our Kincaid, four-post wooden bed, with my arm propped up on a fluffy pillow, I struggled with the concepts in the pages. C.S. Lewis is a brilliant writer. I had to stay focused and concentrate to mentally digest the material. Learning from this intellectual and godly man is why I chose to read it, but his book was not light bedtime reading.

After chewing on a couple of chapters in bed, I was joined by my hubby. He, too, loved to read in bed. Before falling asleep, I looked up. To my surprise, I saw a vision of two little things moving around. I squinted to clear my eyes, but they did not disappear. Before my eyes, one figure faded away, leaving only one. As quick as it had appeared, the vision was gone. What did I just see? Leaning over to my best friend, I said, "Honey, did you see what I saw?" He replied, "What did you see?" I told him, and he inquisitively replied, "No." Bewildered, amazed, and astonished were a few of the adjectives to describe my state of mind that evening. I tried reading some more, but my mind kept wandering back to the vision on the ceiling. What did it mean and why did I see it when my husband did not? What was I to do with it? The answers to these questions eluded me like a riddle without an explanation. Eventually, I fell off into a deep sleep.

Morning came and it unveiled a gorgeous winter day. The sleep renewed my mind and body. Before I rolled out of bed, Andy had already showered and was off fighting the teeming Toronto traffic. Still pregnant and feeling yucky, I started my morning routine. Our sweet little Canadian cats always followed me to my bathroom. This day, my two-legged little ones were also not far behind.

Sorry, but I need to be graphic in this part of the story so you do not miss any of the important details. So, reader beware! Here goes …

I sat on the commode feeling as if I needed to relieve myself. For some strange reason, a few small pieces of connected toilet paper were floating untouched on the top of the water in the toilet bowl. I did not notice it until I had finished my business. Something happened physically and it was not my "regular morning routine," if you know what I mean. I turned and looked down into the commode to investigate. There laid a perfectly shaped fetus. I could not hold back the tears that flooded my eyes. Christiana, who was just four years old, came in and tried to comfort me. She asked what had happened. I explained that I had lost the baby I was carrying inside me. Now, we were both bawling while I was kneeling by the toilet. By this time, my little guy walked in to join us. Luke was not quite sure what was going on. He was under two years old at the time. Lukey saw that we were distraught over something in the toilet, so he did instinctively what a man would do: fix the problem. He walked up to the beige porcelain toilet and pulled down the silver lever. In a flush, it was gone. The fetus, the beginning of my future child, was gone. Eleven weeks into the pregnancy and that little one disappeared. My daughter, sobbing, asked, "Why did this happen, momma?" Choking back my tears, trying to be strong, I replied, "I don't know."

Then, I remembered the strange vision I had the night before. The previous night I could not tell what the two little moving things were. At this point, I shared my thoughts with Christiana, "Perhaps, they were babies, and maybe, just maybe, there was one more still inside of me." My daughter understood what I shared. At such a young age, Christiana could comprehend that God had given me the vision to prepare me for what was to come. I knew what I was saying would be hard for the doctors to comprehend. One might think I had lost my senses. However, it was worth the risk. I had to tell them so they could check for the possibility of a twin.

Quickly, I called my husband and then the doctor's office. The nurse said to come in right away. Jeni showed up to watch my kids, and I departed to the doctor's office. They worked me into the schedule, and I saw the male doctor. I did not know him very well, but I understood he was a believer. He checked my body and said I had a complete miscarriage. Humbly, I asked, "Is there any chance I could have been carrying twins?" His answer started to make me doubt, "He said there is no sign of another fetus in your body." But I knew what I saw in the vision which required me to speak up.

"Please listen to me, and know I am sane," is how I started to tell the doctor. "Last night while reading, I saw a vision on the ceiling of my bedroom. It was two small moving objects side by side. One faded away and one remained. Then, the vision ended. Please, if there is any chance I could be pregnant with another child, I need to know." Perplexed and a bit doubtful, he prescribed an ultrasound. As I was leaving, he said, "Do not be disappointed if you find out that I am correct. At least you will know for sure." I thanked him for not discounting me as an insane woman and allowing me to have a more conclusive answer. However, his words brought significant doubt to my mind. I was suffering from a painful loss, and he did not give me much hope for a second child in my womb.

Returning home, I made my way up the grey stained carpet which lined the stairs, and I crawled into my son's room. There I wept some more. Maybe I was wrong. Fresh snow lay on the ground, calling my name. Perhaps we should head to the slopes and go skiing this weekend to take our minds off the unbearable pain. Should I go to the appointment on Monday or blow it off? I needed to decide: to have hope or to not have hope.

After much mental and emotional struggle, I chose to have hope. That weekend our family excitedly donned our winter clothes, including our mittens, hats, and boots. We built a couple of snowmen and two forts in the yard. A giant snowball fight followed with the little ones. Girls against boys! We had a blast, and I did not risk skiing while possibly still pregnant with the second twin.

Monday rolled around and more doubt tried to creep into my mind. However, I was steadfast. I went to the appointment, undressed, donned the green robe, sat with my feet up, and waited for the radiologist. While patiently waiting, I prayed silently. Here I go again, opening my mouth and expecting criticism. Regardless, I decided to tell the radiologist what had transpired last Thursday night and Friday morning. Ultimately, I wanted her to know what to look for and possibly validate what I saw in the vision. In addition, while I lay in the six-by-eight-foot examination room on the chilly Monday morning, I remembered I woke up thinking, maybe, just maybe, the Lord could use this unfortunate situation for His glory, by leading the radiologist to Jesus.

She listened to me as she did her job. Vaginal ultrasounds are truly no fun, but I will never forget this one. As I told her the story, she commented, "I do not understand all that you are telling me, but I do see a healthy baby growing inside of you. All the measurements show your child to be about eleven weeks." This time, tears of joy began to roll down my face. God had shown me the vision. Those two little things were indeed my babies. He was preparing me for what was to come. I could not stop praising Him for His goodness and His love for my family. The location of that telling appointment was but a mere mile from our house. I solemnly walked to that appointment. The return trip was much more fun, skipping all the way home. I could not wait to tell my man and our children that I was still pregnant. I had been carrying twins!

15

A LIFE SET STRAIGHT

"Lord, You are such a good and loving God, please help my dear friend overcome this horrible vice."

The home phone rang three times before I picked up the call. Typically, I would not answer a phone call while studying the Word. This time was different. The South African accent came tentatively through the earpiece. I knew it had to be my new friend, Pauline, from our homemakers home church. We had an immediate connection. I gave her a friendly Texas greeting, "Howdy girl!" She did not return the lightheartedness. Instead, this dear friend stumbled to express herself. It was apparent to me that she was not in a jovial mood. Pauline had called for a true friend. One who would not judge her, but a friend who would support and help her. I am not quite sure why she chose me, but I am glad she did. Her voice quivered as she asked, "Can I trust you?" I answered, "Of course." She proceeded to tell me that she was ashamed of what she was doing and wanted to get it off her chest. I reminded her that we have a loving and forgiving God.

Those words must have been what Pauline needed to hear. After a long pause, she began to speak. I listened intently as she shared that she—this wife and mother of two—had a deep, dark secret. For years she had been addicted to pornography. This was a new situation for me. She needed help, a friend—and the Lord to show up in a big way. After listening to all she had to share, I suggested a simple prayer. It went something like this, *"Lord, You are such a good and loving God, please help my dear friend overcome this horrible vice."* While praying for her, I knew she needed to talk to our pastor to receive desperately needed counseling. My friend needed freedom from this sin that had so easily entangled her.

I was so happy that Pauline accepted the suggestion to talk with our pastor, uncover her sin, and ask for help. She had already prayed with me and had asked God Almighty for forgiveness. I remember telling her, "God will use this for His glory. One day, you will be proclaiming your freedom and healing from this sin so others will receive freedom too." My dear friends, that is exactly what happened. Our pastor plugged her into an online site that the Lord used to set her free. After completing the program and succeeding with flying colors, she became a leader in helping others receive freedom from their sexual addiction to pornography. God is so good!

—

I will never forget the Christmas card I received from Pauline that season. There was so much joy exuding from the vibrant family picture. I called her shortly after receiving the brilliant card to catch up and hear the fantastic news! Another captive had been set free! Free indeed!

16

A LIFE FOUND

"Lord, help me lead Jeni to You."

Remember my employee who became a friend, Jeni? She became much more than just a friend because God had a divine appointment with her. The day started as any typical day. Jeni promptly arrived at nine in the morning, then I retreated to the cold, slate floor in the sunroom to dig into the Word. The time flew by. Before I knew it, it was lunchtime. Moving to the kitchen to enjoy my kids' company, I invited Jeni to sit down with us. After chowing down a light lunch, the little ones retreated to the playroom. We could see their activity as Jeni began to ask me some serious questions.

I wish I could remember exactly how the conversation evolved. I remember Jeni being curious about why I always retreated to my quiet place in the sunroom. What was I studying? Why did I like it so much? I remember thinking, "This could be the moment I get to share my faith with her." So, I prayed a silent, simple prayer, *"Lord, help me lead Jeni to You."* I explained how someone once said that the Creator of the universe wanted to have a relationship with little ol' me. I remembered how that concept blew me away. How could I resist?

After all these years, what sticks most profoundly in my memory was Jeni's erroneous thought that God would not and could not forgive her. She said with such remorse, "What I have done is unforgivable." I responded by explaining that my God is a loving and forgiving God. Again, she reiterated that what she had done was unforgivable. This time, my response was that my God is the God of second chances. Whatever has been done, He will forgive those who sincerely ask for His forgiveness.

I knew my words were not enough to explain all that Christ has done for us and how God Almighty, the Creator of the universe, could forgive our acts that grieve Him. Suddenly, the memory of the training from the Willow Creek Evangelism Conference popped into my head. I quickly grabbed my kids' drawing pad and a pencil. I drew two sides of a mountain separated by a large gorge, much like the Grand Canyon, but on a much simpler scale. The stick figures were the extent of my artistic abilities. I drew a large stick figure and wrote the name G O D over it on the right side of the mountain. On the left side, I drew a couple of small stick figures representing Jeni and me. I shared, "God is perfect, and my imperfections keep me from being in a close relationship with Him. Then, I drew a vertical line down the middle of the deep gorge representing the separation caused by my sin.

I reiterated to Jeni, "God loves you and me and He wants us to be in a close relationship with Him." Next, I drew a line representing a bridge across the gorge connecting the two plateaus. The new horizontal line intersecting the vertical line created the cross. I explained, "As a result of His sacrificial love, He gave up His One and Only Son, Jesus, to die on the cross so we could be in a sweet relationship with Him. The cross is what Jesus hung on to bring us to the other side. As a result, we could be with God the Father, God Almighty." Next, I walked the stick people over the cross-bridge to the other side—to G O D.

Even though Jesus was sinless, He took the penalty of our sin, which is death, that each of us deserved. He did this so we could be in a relationship with Him. He died on the cross and three days later rose from the dead. He defeated the grave! I explained to Jeni, "Your relationship with God Almighty starts now and lasts for eternity."

The lightbulb turned on in this bright young lady's head and she broke down in tears. Jeni said, "So what I did, aborting my second child, is forgivable?" I said, "Yes, and I am so sorry you had to go through that." The Chinese Communist Government strongly encourages, if not demands, one child per couple. Their son was the only one allowed to be born into their family. My heart broke for her. She wept and then prayed after me to ask God Almighty for forgiveness and for Him to be her heavenly Father. I assured her that He forgave her and that He loved her. The holy angels were singing in the throne room after that prayer! Jeni became my new sister in Christ. That day was very special for her and for me.

17

DOUBLE LOSS

*"Lord, if this is Your good and
perfect will, let us hear a heartbeat."
"Jesus, help me, please!"
"I can't take this (emotional) pain any
longer, take it from me."*

The brisk cold air covered the large glass windows with
crooked lines of white frost, reminding us of the northern
tundra we had moved to just eleven months prior. It was
our first Canadian Christmas, and our tradition of having family

visit was extra special that year. My mom and dad, Joan, and Harry, came to celebrate with us, making the trek in their tried-and-true, off-white station wagon with imitation wood panels. It was my dad's favorite hunting vehicle. When they arrived, the warmth and love of my parents filled our enormous, stone-cold rental home.

Celebrating Christ's birth at the evening service at our new church, The Meeting House, was extra special with my parents. They raised me in the Lutheran church back in Sterling, Illinois. Now, we were worshipping and serving at a non-denominational church with Mennonite roots in Ontario, Canada. Boy, things had changed.

Waking up Christmas morning, I noticed something subtly different. The odd and somewhat disturbing vibration I had felt all over my body during this pregnancy had mysteriously disappeared that morning. I remember sitting with my parents on the ebony-stained oak floors enjoying a cup of hot tea while our kids excitedly opened presents under the tree. I thought, *how odd?* This was the first time in almost four and a half months that I could enjoy a cup of caffeine without throwing up. Maybe, just maybe, I was out of the woods and the rest of the pregnancy was going to be a breeze. My hopes were high.

As lovely as it was to see my parents arrive and enjoy the holidays, it was sad to see them go when my dad had to return to work. Their old Buick became smaller and smaller as my father drove it down the road. I watched it disappear as it reached the turn on to the main road. The next turn put them on the Queen Elizabeth Way highway headed to the border. Back on our own, in a foreign land, I thought, *we can do this!*

New Year's Eve arrived with my belly bulging. It was time for my eighteen-week checkup! Off I went to my Canadian doctor's office to have my regularly scheduled visit. The first stop was the waiting room. Before I could relax again, I needed to step onto the dreaded scale. The next stop was the examination room. Finally, a nurse greeted me and asked how I was doing. "Great!" I replied.

"No more strange vibrations all over my body, and I can finally enjoy a cup of tea in the morning without feeling sick." *I've got this,* so I thought. The nurse continued her examination. "Let me check your temperature … good, it is normal. Next, I need to check your blood pressure. Good, it is also normal," she said as she annotated this information in her notes. "Now for the good stuff! Let's take a listen to your baby's heartbeat," she stated excitedly.

The nurse placed the stethoscope on my belly. She moved it around. "Hmm," she lightly sighed. "I cannot seem to find the baby's heartbeat." Surely, she just had not found the perfect spot. I adjusted my position a bit for her to get another listen. Abruptly, she left the room. Next, the doctor entered and did the same. She said, "Not to worry," but she wanted me to go next door to the hospital to have an ultrasound done right away to see how the baby was doing. I was very concerned as I gently rubbed my enlarged tummy. The medical group that was taking care of me and my baby did not even know I was carrying twins the first eleven weeks of this pregnancy. Now, they could not find the heartbeat. I prayed, *"Lord, if this is Your good and perfect will, let us hear a heartbeat."* I could not have imagined what I was about to go through.

My hubby agreed to meet me at the hospital. I called Jeni, and she stayed longer than usual with our kiddos so I could have this now-extended checkup. Thankfully, she was happy to stay and help. I called my friend Heather to let her know things were not right and to pray. She reached out to Beth, one of our beloved pastors, to pray.

The hospital received me right away. I walked into a temporary examination room where the walls consisted of light blue cloth hung over metal pipes. A pleasant attendant rolled the ultrasound machine into the close quarters. Someone spread a cold clear, jelly-like substance over my extended tummy. Then they took meticulous measurements of the baby. Still, no heartbeat. The second baby had made it to eighteen weeks of new life, just not yet born.

The out-of-reach OB-GYN finally made himself known. He was a well-educated, thin Asian man. He was well respected in his field and especially at this hospital. The doctor said the baby would need to be delivered as it had died in utero. I had two options: be admitted into the hospital and induce the delivery or go home and wait for it to happen naturally. Eventually, my body would no longer welcome the dead baby. I would have to deliver it one way or the other because the pregnancy was too far along to perform a dilation and curettage procedure without harming me. Tears began to flow from my eyes. Thoughts raced through my mind. How could this be? I lost one baby. Now, just seven weeks later, how could I lose the second baby? Then I remembered the vision given to me the night before I lost the first twin. The two images were in the air wiggling about and then one disappeared. Shortly thereafter, the second one vanished. I assumed the vision had ended. I did not realize it was the end of the second baby too. Oh, the pain, the grief, the shock, and the double loss was overwhelming.

The emotional day turned into a horrific New Year's Eve. Delivering a dead baby was not how I intended to spend our night celebrating the new year. Nothing had prepared me to bring in 2001 with a second traumatic loss.

Quickly, I made the painful decision to deliver. I could not fathom the idea of waiting around for my body to naturally expel this unborn child inside of me. Next, they wheeled me upstairs to the labor and delivery floor. The doctor came in and explained they would administer Pitocin to start the delivery. No pain killers, such as an epidural, were discussed. The main goal was to induce the labor. The discomfort grew in my lower back. Before I knew it, I was having contractions. I just kept praying for the Lord to take my pain. He was so sweet to bless me with some fantastic, godly nurses who held my hand and prayed with me and for me. It was getting late, and Jeni had to head home. As a result, my hubby had to leave me to take care of our kids. I was on my own in this depressing delivery room.

Never will I forget the beautiful tiny baby that came out of me. Perfect, yet lifeless. She had all ten fingers and all ten toes. What could have gone wrong? Why would she not make it to breathe her first breath? I did not drink nor smoke. I even cut out caffeine during the first part of the pregnancy. I did not have much time to lament over this sweet child. The nurses quickly took her and replaced my soaked three-foot-by-three-foot pad with a fresh one. The new year rang in, and I was bleeding out. I summoned for my nurse and showed her my second soaked pad. She was surprised at how fast it had filled. She quickly changed it and put another one underneath me. I was in excruciating pain, to say the least: emotional pain and physical pain. When I delivered the baby, the placenta did not fully detach. As a result, a portion of it remained inside of me wreaking havoc. The nurse ran to get the doctor who checked on me. He quickly assessed the situation. The nurse changed yet another blood-soaked pad. The doc promptly scrubbed his hands, put gloves on, and reached deep into my insides. I screamed as he cleaned me out like a pumpkin being turned into a jack-o-lantern by ripping out all the pumpkin seeds attached to the inside lining of the gourd. The nurse grabbed my hand as I cried out, *"Jesus, help me, please!"*

The abrupt and painful procedure helped to end the extensive loss of blood. I could not wait for the morning's light and the much-needed familiar face of my hubby. The physical pain was ending, but the emotional pain had only begun. Less than twenty-four hours later, I was headed back to our cold rental home. I really needed to be heading home to Texas, to our friends who were like family. The loss of the second baby was the breaking point for me. I told Andy, "You need to get me back home to Sugar Land, as soon as possible!" I was done. But I knew moving home would not happen overnight. It would be six months before we loaded up the moving truck and headed back to Sugar Land.

After returning to our rental home from the delivery, I pretty much cried my way through each day for the next three days. My tears were flowing like a leaking faucet. In fact, it was hard to get myself out of my bed. The loss was overwhelming. On the third day of emotional distress, I cried out to my God, *"Lord, I can't take this (emotional) pain any longer; take it from me!"* At that very moment of crying out, I could feel the emotional pain that had consumed me begin to lift. It was genuinely supernatural! The Lord had delivered me from my emotional pain. The very next day, one of my sisters called to check on me. She asked, "How are you?" I told her, "I am great." Perplexed, she replied, "You do not have to be so strong." I truthfully said, "I am doing well." Supernatural healings are remarkable!

18

RETURN TO
TEXAS - GRACE

"Lord, may I start a home church at our church, CUMC?

The snow had melted away, new birth began to spring up, and school was quickly coming to an end. It was time to say our goodbyes. Our Discipleship Bible Study ended with the special baptism of our once apostate friend, Grace. Our home church was taking a break for the summer but not without the baptism of our new and beloved friend, Tanja, the Messianic

Jew. It was such a blessing to be able to see these two precious souls fall in love with the Word—Jesus.

The Meeting House gave us the sweetest send off. Just thinking about how much we grew spiritually, emotionally, and biblically—and with such amazing people—makes me grateful and joyful. Boy, our experience was very different from what our Texas pastor had shared, "Canada is a country without God." What a relief it was that we discovered quite the opposite! During the year and a half we attended our Canadian church, the Meeting House, it probably doubled or tripled in attendance. We launched a remote campus for others to come to know the truth and grow closer to the Lord without traveling to Oakville to receive the teaching and be in Christian fellowship. The Meeting House has and will always have a special place in my heart.

Our welcome back home to Sugar Land was sweet! Our beloved friend, Judi, helped us celebrate our daughter's fifth birthday. Christiana benefited by celebrating with both her friends in Canada and our dear friends back home. I was happy to return and pick up with the friendships we had left behind. Upon arriving in Sugar Land, we also returned to our former church, Christ United Methodist Church (CUMC). The Lord had put a special place in my heart for home churches, so I prayed and asked God Almighty, *"Lord, may I start a home church at our church, CUMC?"* God is so good! He answered my simple prayer when Pastor Tom gave us the greenlight to start a women's small group, or home church as they called it, in Canada. Gloria, who was my very first Bible study leader for Discipleship I, and I had the pleasure of teaming up to lead this new group. What a blessing it is to learn and share wherever God takes us in His good and perfect will.

—

The month we returned home, Andy had business in Austin. I wanted to surprise my hubby. So, being spontaneous, I packed an overnight bag, placed the kids in their car seats, and drove three hours to the capital of Texas. My heart desired to have another child. Andy was on board, and it did not take long to fulfill that desire. The last-minute trip did the trick, and I became pregnant! What a joy! What a surprise! We could not wait. We discussed names during a trip to Galveston while sitting on the sandy beach with our best friends. If she were to be a girl, she would be called Grace. The name was fitting because it was by God's grace that we would have another child after losing the twins in the past twelve months. God is so good and so gracious!

19

LOVE VERSUS HATE

"Lord, what should we do?"

Our old church was calling us back to Sugar Land. Initially, I reached out to our pastor and raved about the extraordinary spiritual growth we experienced while living in the country to our north. I let him know that God was not dead in Canada. In fact, we found quite the opposite while attending our Canadian church. Pastor Tom was amazed by all that had transpired in such a short period of eighteen months. I excitedly told him about the women's home church I was a part of and how I wanted to bless CUMC with this type of awesome fellowship. He was interested in what I was pitching. After experiencing such solid, godly connections with the Canadian women while growing in the Word, how could I not want to start a women's home church at CUMC? Pastor Tom was onboard, and we began to get the word out by personal invitation and the church bulletin.

I will never forget our first meeting. The day started as expected, with me rising to a cup of hot coffee and praying. Eagerly, I moved to the shower and picked out clothes for our first women's small group meeting. How exciting! Hair dried and a little eyeliner applied: check. Bible in hand: check. Notebook with contacts of our ladies and a loose plan for the first semester: check. Purse and keys: check. As I drove north on U.S. Highway 59 to the home of our hostess, Sharon, my cell phone rang. It was my dear friend, Kim, who was also joining the women's group. She had a concerned tone in her voice that I recognized right away. Let me explain why I knew there was an issue.

Kim and I had the pleasure of attending the same college my freshman year. She was my beloved biology lab partner. I had transferred after my first year because of the internship opportunity at IBM in Chicago. We had lost touch for years. But God is so kind. He reunited us at my first branch meeting when I transferred to IBM Houston. I remember Andy, my fiancé at the time, exclaiming, "You must meet my friend, Kim. She is so much like you. You will love her." Funny thing, she had and still has way more energy than me and probably many more MIPs. In the technology world, a MIP is what we call intelligence or the ability to process a lot of information at once. She was and still is an energizer bunny. I ended up playing softball with Kim on the IBM team. I affectionally nicknamed her Kimmie. We even moved to the same neighborhood and ended up running the Greatwood Women's Club together. I do not know how we found the time, but I remember our motive was to add more Christmas decorations to our then growing neighborhood. We loved to rollerblade around the community together. We were young and full of life!

Back to the untimely phone call. As soon as I answered, Kimmie demanded, "Where are you?" I noted, "I am on 59, headed north. Where are you?" She declared in her heightened voice, "I am at my doctor's office for my OB appointment watching the news. Have you seen what happened?" I quickly answered, "No, I am driving. What are you referring to?" Kim explained the daunting news that a Boeing 747 airplane had flown into one of the twin towers in New York City. "What?" I announced in dismay. Wanting more clarification, I asked, "What are you talking about?" "You are not going to believe your eyes!" declared my very pregnant friend. "Are we still going to meet to start the women's home church?" she questioned. I prayed with my eyes wide open and my heart hurting to hear this startling and horrific news, *"Lord, what should we do?"* I knew without a shadow of a doubt we were still supposed to meet. By the time my co-leader, Gloria, reached me, I already knew the answer to her impending question.

Our first meeting was planned to be filled with fun, food, and introductions. We had loosely laid out a plan as to what we would study for the semester. Our intent was to discuss study options and finalize our plans. We wanted the women to begin to get to know one another. Bringing twelve ladies together is no small feat. Some had known each other well. Others did not have any prior knowledge of each other until our first meeting. Our plan was foiled on September 11, 2001.

But God ordained our meeting to pray for our country and all those affected by this horrific terrorist attack. So that is precisely what we did.

Fear was ramped up that day in our country. What about our kids? I remember the decision I had to make to leave our kids at school and church or pick them up and take them to the safety of our home. I had peace about leaving them where they were. Uprooting them at that moment would only disturb their new routine. The overall tone of our meeting was one of dismay and broken hearts, yet it was an endearing time of prayer for others. Our lives were already being knitted together more tightly than I could have ever orchestrated, all caused by the enemy's plan and executed by the hate-filled Islamic terrorists.

20

THINGS FRAMED UP

"Lord, please give me a friend to sit with today."

Remember my new friend, Chung, from the frame shop? He was the young man I had been praying for to come to know our sweet Jesus. He had explained to me that he was at a crossroads. He had become emotionally involved with a young lady he was dating. I knew what he was trying to communicate. For this reason, I shared with him that sexual sin is a dangerous and slippery slope. Once on it, it's hard to get off of it. I prayed and prayed for him to come to know the Lord and to stay off that slippery slope. Before moving to Canada, I never learned if he had chosen to follow Christ or the world's ways. Having said that, God is so sweet. He wanted me to know that my prayers for Chung did not go unanswered. Let me explain.

While driving to pick up my daughter at the small, godly Lutheran school, I heard on the Christian radio station that Willow Creek Community Church (WCCC) was coming to the Houston area for an evangelism conference. Oh, my goodness! I was excited! This church was the church that I attended after accepting Jesus as my Lord and Savior at eighteen years old. Remember my friend, Crew, who told me the truth? The truth is that the Creator of the universe wanted to have a relationship with little ol' me. Willow Creek was the church we attended together, and they held the first evangelism conference I eagerly attended to equip myself for leading our evangelism team at CUMC in Sugar Land. Therefore, these thoughts raced through my mind: Would I get to hear some of the same pastors teach again? Whom else would I get to listen to and learn from? I could not wait to sign up for this event. I wondered, *who would go with me?* I did not care if I went by myself because I knew I needed to attend.

You guessed it. I could not find anyone to commit the time to attend this conference with me. I went alone. Well, not entirely alone. When you have Jesus, you always have a close friend with you.

The drive to the Woodlands, which is in the north part of Houston, was long but relatively easy. My praise music was loud enough to drown out my less-than-glorious singing voice. As I was parking the car, I quietly asked, *"Lord, please give me a friend to sit with today."* Little did I know, He had an entire group of people for me to sit with and enjoy!

The large church auditorium was packed. I am guessing it sat anywhere from 500 to 700 people. I found my way to an open seat and made myself at home. Looking around, I noticed a group of youthful Koreans. It was apparent that they were all together. You could tell they had a sweet and respectful relationship with one another. At the break, I leaned over and introduced myself. I have no earthly idea why I made the introduction. Maybe because I admired their friendship? Their love for one another was evident. Perhaps I introduced myself because they reminded me of my friend, Chung? Who knows? One young lady, Eun ae, stood out to me. She seemed to be the spiritually mature leader of the group and unafraid to speak to a stranger like me. We engaged in a meaningful conversation, and at one point I asked if they all attended the same church. Eun ae confirmed that they all attended the same Korean-speaking church and were very close.

On a whim, I inquired if she had ever met a young man named Chung. I explained that he had worked at a frame shop in Sugar Land and had helped me select frames for my child's pictures. Her reaction was one I will never forget. She excitedly questioned, "Are you the woman that shared the love of Christ with Jon Chung, gave him Christian music, and told him to be careful regarding sexual sin?" My thoughts were racing. Wow! These lovely people are tightly knit. I responded, "Yes, that was me," as I thought, *oh, my goodness, what a small world.* Next, Eun ae excitedly disrupted everyone else's conversations to announce who I was to the rest of the group. They were just as thrilled as she was. They gave me hugs, high-fives, and loads of smiles. She went on to explain the sweetest news I have ever heard. Chung was in Ukraine on a mission helping orphans. He did it! He took the plunge and went full-on for Jesus! What a good and gracious God He is for allowing me to know this fantastic news. My gracious God answered my simple, sweet, heartfelt prayers. I could not stop smiling for days. The joy from the Lord is stupendous!

A couple of years earlier, I had begun to diligently ask the Lord to allow me to lead someone to Christ. I had prayed earnestly for

Chung. Now he was in the Kingdom and serving so faithfully. We never know when we plant a seed if it will take root and grow. Eun ae took my phone number and address and shared them with Chung. Approximately a month later, I received the sweetest, most inspired letter from him. Upon opening the envelope, I felt the presence of the Holy Spirit roll off the pages. I have never experienced a more Holy Spirit-filled letter in my entire life. My brother in Christ expressed overwhelming love and gratitude. I praise God for allowing me to be used by Him, for His Glory, in that little frame shop. Jesus had it all framed up.

21

ANOTHER BLESSING AND ANOTHER TEST

"Lord, if it is Your good and perfect
will, I would like another child."
"Lord, Your will be done regarding this child's name."

"Lord, if it is Your will, let me know and give us unity."

Grace was such an easy delivery. One, two, three, and—voila, Grace was born! Laying on the delivery bed, I asserted that I was ready for another blessing. The doctors and nurses were surprised at my desire for another child! I had told my hubby before marriage that I wanted a large family. Mostly because I was the caboose of six kids. Had my parents stopped after their fifth child, I would not be here. My hubby must have forgotten that conversation because he said we were done having babies after three of these fantastic gifts. I knew better than to argue with him. I just took my request to the Lord. *"Lord, if it is Your good and perfect will, I would like another child."*

Two years and five months later, God answered my simple prayer, and our baby boy was born one month premature. Name? Hmm … he was one month early and was our blessing number four. He was born and we had no name for him. At that time, the book of Joshua had become one of my favorite books in the Bible. What a mighty warrior for the Lord! My husband wanted to name him Jake or Jacob. Jacob was a deceiver in the Bible whom God renamed Israel. Jake is short for Jacob. Instead of arguing to determine the child's name, we cast lots, a practice often described in the Bible to resolve conflicts or understand God's will. Andy wrote down the three names: Joshua, Jacob, and Jake. Then he cut the paper into three pieces. Into the hat they went. We prayed a simple prayer, *"Lord, Your will be done regarding this child's name."* We agreed whichever name pulled first would be the baby's first name. Whichever name was pulled second from the hat would become his middle name. Andy was a bit frustrated when he drew Joshua first. Then I pulled Jacob. Joshua Jacob became his name. We saved the name Jake for one of our beloved, furry, four-legged pets.

Given Joshua's early arrival into this world, the Neonatal Intensive Care Unit, NICU, became his temporary home. Every day, I went to the hospital and nursed my little guy. During the evening, I pumped white gold to provide breast milk for the nurses to feed him the next night. It seemed like forever before we could bring Joshua Jacob home from the NICU. Many people prayed for that little man. In time, he joined the Langsam gang!

The ride home from the hospital was uneventful. As soon as we got Joshua into the car, however, we noticed him wheezing. How could this be? We had never heard this sound before. Consequently, we decided to keep him close that evening and call our pediatrician in the morning. She referred us to a specialist who diagnosed Joshua with Laryngomalacia. This foreign word meant that Joshua had a damaged larynx. Surgery was out of the question on such a tiny newborn, especially since the odds were in his favor to outgrow it.

—

School was back in session. Two of our four kids were now attending the school we adored, Faith Lutheran. During this time, we had felt a strong call to join a new church, Crossbridge, which was just getting started. New birth! It was extremely difficult to get our minds around leaving CUMC, but we knew the prompting we had received to go and help with this new church plant was from the Lord. A couple that we had become friends with were involved in this new church's prayer ministry. They were moving to Austin due to a work transfer and wanted me to consider volunteering to help lead the prayer ministry. Of course, I said, "I would pray about it." After prayer, it was evident that this is where the Lord wanted me to serve.

Around that time, the pastor's wife, Kathleen, invited me to join in a women's Bible study. The author was a local Bible study teacher, Beth Moore. Her format of study was a new concept to me. I had not yet had the opportunity to participate in any of her Bible studies. Kathleen told me how the study worked, and it sounded good to me. The study was called *Jesus the One and Only.* It was a remarkable in-depth study of God's Word. I learned so much from spending time in the Word. Beth Moore writes studies primarily for women that require about twenty to thirty minutes of homework each day in her workbooks. The daily study traverses a lot of scripture, both Old and New Testaments. After five days of some serious work, it's time to rest and then get back together with the group to watch video-based teaching on the subject. I fell in love with Jesus all over again.

—

Shortly after bringing our newest Langsam home from the hospital, my husband began to express his desire to make a career change. A company in Florida was very interested in hiring him. He prayed about it. I pretty much said, "No way!" After just having a newborn baby who spent many nights in the NICU, I wanted no part of another stressful life decision that would mean moving halfway across the United States. Thank goodness, Andy did not push the issue. He told the president of the company that he could not move right now and thanked them for the opportunity. The next day, while reading the Bible study, God reminded me from His Word to support my husband. Oh, my heart sank. Andy wanted to take that position as the Vice President of Sales in a start-up company, but I would not even consider it. The reason I did not want to consider the career change is because we had made an enormous mistake once before by moving for the wrong reasons: more money, promotion, cars, etc. I was not budging this time unless I knew it was God's good and perfect will. I prayed something like this, *"Lord, if it is Your will, let me know and give us unity."*

Immediately after my heartfelt prayer, I felt the Lord nudging me to call my hubby to let him know what I prayed for and to get his input. Once I made it to the pickup car line at our children's school, I called Andy and shared the concern of my heart and my desire to support him. He said, "I really appreciate you supporting me. I think it is time to make a career change. I feel it is God's will." We hung up the phone and he called the company's president, Jason. Soon thereafter, Andy called me back and told me they had given the job to someone else. The answer was quick. I thought, *Phew! Yay, I obeyed, and now I get to stay in Houston. Thank you, Jesus!*

However, the story gets better. Jason called Andy back and said, "I spoke with the board, and we want you to join us even though we filled the Vice President of Sales position. If I can get it approved, would you consider the position of Chief Operating Officer?" Jason's response floored my hubby. God is so good, and He had a better plan for Andy. Praying through the decision with the right motives resulted in a greater position and a much more fulfilling career path for my hubby.

22

MISSING ONE

"God, please help me!"
"Lord, we need Your help to find Christiana."

The crisp, cold January weather had settled in. Christmas lights were down. The seasons had changed, and it was time for us to move along. With much expectation, we loaded the blue Chrysler minivan with our three kids, our newborn baby, and my sweet mom affectionately known as

Grandma Joan. We headed east to the Sunshine State. Andy was at the helm. My mom was co-pilot. Josh was in the infant car seat, buckled into the bucket seat, and I sat in the adjacent seat. Our three oldest packed into the third row. Every seat in the minivan was filled.

Our beloved Canadian cats, Miss Lucky, and Tiger had free rein in the vehicle while we humans buckled up. I can only imagine how interesting we looked at the pit stops. What a spectacle! One, two, three, four—are there more? Five, six, seven humans of all shapes and sizes came pouring out of the car. We were in a hurry to get there, so pit stops were just a place to stretch and hit the bathrooms. Eating meals in the minivan was not only allowed but necessary to make the twenty-four-hour trip as quick as possible. Even ordering fast food at the drive-through establishments became comical. The vehicle began to have an odor of its own. Somehow, we survived and made it to our hold-over destination, the Disney World Animal Kingdom Hotel.

What were we thinking when we planned a Disney pit stop in the middle of this massive move across half of our glorious country? Three days at Disney World was even more exhausting! We did it because we wanted to give our oldest children something to look forward to when we moved away from their beloved friends and sweet, Christian school. Christiana was in the middle of third grade, and Luke was in the middle of first grade. Grace had not yet started preschool. Josh was only four months old.

Leaving Texas (again) with the promise to return in five years was the saving grace. This time, we had thoroughly prayed through the decision to move. Remember our previous mistake when we accepted a move to Canada without seeking God's will? Even though God taught us so much while living in Mississauga, Canada, it was also a very trying, emotional time for me and our family.

After praying through the decision to move to Florida, I had peace amid the unknown. However, it did not take away the pain of leaving friends who were like family. My goal was to establish new roots while maintaining friendships back in Sugar Land. I wanted to be used by the Lord no matter where we called home.

Somehow, we survived the three-day pit stop at Disney. Only a three-hour drive remained to reach our new home. The semi-truck filled with all our personal belongings—our furniture, boxes upon boxes, and Andy's car—showed up shortly after we finished the walk-through of our new home. The unloading and unpacking chaos began before I could say shazam! Indeed, it was a bustling, busy day. The masculine movers dumped everything from the truck into our clean, empty home. We worked as hard as we could to make up all the beds so everyone could sleep in their own bed that first night. However, as the evening approached, we realized we were missing someone.

Josh was in the bassinet by our bed. Grace and Luke were asleep in their beds. Where was our oldest? Fear struck me! Oh, my God! Where was she? I asked myself. "Mom, have you seen Christiana?" I asked Andy with fear and trembling in my voice, "Who would take a seven-year-old girl?" The thought raced through my mind: *What a horrible place this is. How can this be, Lord?* I yelled, "Christiana! Christiana!" I screamed at the top of my lungs, running around the house looking frantically for her. Andy and Grandma Joan again checked the bedrooms and couches. I ran outside, hollering as loud as I could for her. My precious baby was gone! Where, oh, where had she gone? *"God, please help me!"* I cried out.

It was time to dial 9-1-1! We could not find Christiana anywhere. My mom, in faith, stopped and prayed. She prayed a simple prayer, *"Lord, we need your help to find Christiana."* The next thing I remember, my mom called me with good news from our master bedroom. She quickly explained, "Even though Christiana was in a deep sleep, miraculously, she sat up from under the covers and then laid back down. It was as though an invisible person slowly lifted her up to a sitting position and then gently laid her back down—so I could see her." Praise God! My mom prayed from the middle of my bedroom and watched Him answer that prayer to find Christiana! Oh, what a sweet relief to have found her. I know who sat her up and laid her back down. I am sure the directive came from the one who sees and hears our prayers, El Roi! Another simple and heartfelt prayer answered miraculously.

23

WHERE HAVE YOU BROUGHT ME?

"Whoa, Lord, where have You brought me?"

The 18-wheel moving truck departed quickly. By the time I made my way upstairs, I noticed mountains of boxes all over our new home. Unbelievably, the unpacking service we hired did not include putting anything away. They simply dumped the boxes and hit the road. Weeks before loading the semi-truck for the Sunshine State, I had purged a large mound of junk and piled it on our driveway to be picked up by our garbage men. The heap was probably seven feet wide and five feet high. Moreover, I was so upset with the thought of leaving all my beloved friends again that I accidentally hit my thumb with the flat head of a hammer. With a throbbing thumb added to the amount of work it took to move a family of six people, I felt overwhelmed. Andy was busy working, so preparing for the movers fell squarely on my shoulders. In addition, Josh at this point would have been only three months old if he had not arrived an entire month early. This nursing, moving mother was completely exhausted.

Our new home sat on a large property in a sleepy neighborhood. Unfortunately, we were one of only three families in our entire neighborhood with small kids. Our new community was a want-to-be equestrian area set amongst the largest equestrian region in Florida. Our little town hosts the Winter Equestrian Festival every year. January through March is a busy time for the small town with loads of equestrians and their four-legged friends. Furthermore, the snowbirds joined our community every winter, making for a very congested area.

Congested is precisely what Southern Boulevard was on this sunny, winter day. My three big kids started their day at the neighborhood school, Wellington Christian. A few days earlier, I had received a book from a friend that had moved from Sugar Land to Oklahoma. Her gift blessed me. After reading it, I packaged it up to share with another friend who had recently moved. I will tell about this treasured book in the next chapter. I filled Josh's diaper bag, placed him securely in the back seat, and off we went on our little adventure to the post office.

However, on my way to mail the book, I encountered a traffic jam on Southern Boulevard. The congestion on the road was nothing unusual since the road crews were working diligently to widen the two-lane road. Much to my surprise, my little eyes witnessed a woman wanting to enter the congested road from a perpendicular street. She had her blinker on to turn left and was slowly nudging her vehicle into the crawling eastbound traffic. Honk! Honk! Honk! The woman driver heading east rolled down her window. Neither driver was happy with the other nor did they want to acquiesce to the other. The merging driver decided to step on the gas pedal and insert her vehicle without the required safe space. Crunch! My jaw, figuratively, hit the steering wheel. Did I witness one woman ram another woman's car with her car? Yes, I did! "Oh, my goodness," I said to myself, as I waited patiently for the traffic light to change color. As I slowly drove past the woman in the damaged vehicle, I thought to tell her I would testify to what happened. Then I remembered Florida was a no-fault state. In other words, the insurance companies would settle the differences. I did not need to be involved. Plus, I had our four-month-old buckled in the back car seat.

Although our little errand had started rough, we finally arrived at the post office thirty minutes later. Since the trip took quite a bit longer than expected, Josh was a hangry little man. He let his frustration out with his small yet mighty lungs. The parking spot had my name on it, so to speak—no car parked to the left or right of it. I parked in the best spot, closest to the post office, with lots of space to avoid door dings. I climbed into the back, pulled Josh out of his car seat, and proceeded to satisfy his hunger.

Much to my surprise, a car flew into the parking spot to the right of my vehicle. I watched the woman driver fling open her door directly into the side of my car. She did not hesitate to look at the potential damage done. Without wasting time, she proceeded to the post office doors. My head was spinning. Who in their right mind would swing their car door directly into someone else's car door and think nothing of it? Josh was a fast drinker. By the time he finished, the careless woman had headed back to her car. I decided to think the best of her and let her know what she had done. I was hoping she would apologize. Ha, ha, ha! "Excuse me, ma'am. I just wanted to let you know that when you exited your vehicle your door slammed into mine." I am sure

I was very calm and kind. Yet, I was on the receiving end of the opposite of kindness, peppered with exaggerated expletives and comments that I have chosen not to share with you. By her response, one would have thought I had damaged her cherished car, not the other way around. I cried out while trying to hold back the tears. *"Whoa! Lord, where have You brought me?"*

The rudeness did not end there. On the return trip, someone else chose to flip me the bird and unload a mouthful of words at me. Thank goodness I do not read lips. I probably did something wrong, given that I did not know my way around yet. However, there was no mercy for a newcomer's honest mistakes on the road. This flippant individual did not know I was new to the area. I wronged him on the road, and he felt entitled to let me know his angry feelings. Unfortunately, I am not a perfect driver, nor do I always keep my cool regarding other drivers, especially when they put my family in harm's way by their lack of attention behind the wheel. I do believe there is such a thing as righteous anger. Jesus expressed it, as He flipped tables in the courtyard of the temple. He was zealous for his house; it was to be a house of prayer. Whether righteous or not, I felt a lot of anger that day.

Typically, an unrighteous finger would not bring me to tears, but that was the last of three rude incidents on the short trip to the post office. It was the last straw that broke the proverbial camel's back. Home—I wanted to go back to Sugar Land, Texas, where people were sweet and kind! They would patiently wait behind a stopped car at the green light, not honking their horn to get the sleepy, distracted driver to proceed. I was one of those drowsy drivers on a quick trip back to Sugar Land. The stoplight cycled completely through: red, green, yellow, red, and green again. I made my turn to the right. I was amazed that no one showed anger toward me nor honked their horn. I missed living in that town and wondered why we needed to move to a place that did not have that same kind of friendly vibe. However, God had other plans for me and my family as I will uncover in the following chapters. His ways are not our ways.

24

MOVE ON ...

"Lord, should I birth a Just Moved Ministry here in West Palm Beach?"

ood news! Yes, something good came out of all the stress from moving. As I looked through the mail, I was surprised to receive a book sent by a dear friend, Vicki Schleimer, from Christ United Methodist Church in Sugar Land. Oh, how I love to learn from an excellent, heaven-sent book. Upon opening this little brown package, I read the title of this gently used book: *After the Boxes are Unpacked,* by Susan Miller.

This was the second time I had received this book from a beloved friend.

The first chapter unleashed the flood gates of tears and emotions which I could not hold back any longer. It was time I let them out and let the healing begin. I was hurting and clinging to what my husband promised me: only five years in Florida. Then we would return to our friends in Sugar Land who were like family. The story in the first chapter of the book is about when God spoke to Abram and told him to move his family to an unknown place. Yes—God did not tell Abram where he was going, only to pack up his family, animals, and possessions and start moving. At least I knew the location of our move. However, I did not know much about Florida. We set out to learn more about it by spending long weekends and vacations exploring our adoptive state.

The year was 2005, and Florida was booming. People from the North were flooding the Sunshine State. Every turn I took, I ran into someone that had just moved to Florida. The book that was twice sent to me brought me much healing and helped me take root and bloom in Wellington, Florida. I decided this book needed to be in more than just my hands. As a result of the book's impact on my life, I bought a ten-pack. I readily handed them out to people I met and subsequently discussed their moving experiences with them. Those enlightening conversations prompted me to pray, *"Lord, should I birth a Just Moved Ministry here in West Palm Beach?"*

After more prayer, I met with Pastor Brian at our church. He liked the idea of offering a ministry to those who had recently moved to the area. Based on his input, I followed up with a plan to make this ministry a reality. It was not that difficult because the book's author had already created a plan. It just took a willing vessel and a church to make it happen.

25

MORE WARFARE

*"Lord, God Almighty, whatever is not of You,
put it in a spiritual box, seal it with the blood of
Christ, and send it to Jesus to be dealt with."*

D id I mention that I began to pray for the people in my new neighborhood while walking and riding my bike? It was not long before I kept seeing a very oddly dressed woman walking on the sidewalk. In fact, she was always walking toward me as I took my kids to Wellington Christian School. To say my spirit was alarmed would be an understatement. Upon seeing her walk in my direction, I would pray for protection for everyone in my car. Her favorite color had to be black since she always dressed in it from head to toe. Never did I witness her in another color of the rainbow. Her stature was thin and tall. Her height was a façade created by her six-inch black platform shoes and her black bun that elevated her another three inches. She was known as the Witch of Wellington. My simple prayer whenever we would see her or sense her presence was the following: *"Lord, God Almighty, whatever is not of You, put it in a spiritual box, seal it with the blood of Christ and send it to Jesus to be dealt with."*

One memorable night, the Witch of Wellington and two other witches came to visit me in a vision. The Witch of Wellington stayed at a distance, merely observing. The other two witches got up close and personal. In this vision, I was rollerblading in our community. The witch that I had a conversation with was African American and somewhat heavy-set. The other was thin, quiet, and of Asian descent. I cannot remember how the conversation got started. Somehow, I shared the simple gospel message with them. I shared the truth. If we believe in our hearts and confess with our mouths that Jesus Christ is God's Son, then when we ask for forgiveness of our sins, He will forgive us completely.

I vividly remember what happened next and how our conversation ended. The witch that communicated the most stated firmly, "I cannot be forgiven!" I quickly replied, "My God is a good God and a forgiving God. All you have to do is ask for forgiveness and He will forgive you." I put my hands on her upper arms and gave her a warm embrace to let her know I was concerned for her. Then, I looked her in the eye to affirm that I was sincere and truthful. I thought maybe she would believe me because she chose to come see me. The moment my hands touched her I knew the reason for the pain she was suffering, that which was at the root of her unbelief. I knew she had an abortion and could not forgive herself. If she could not forgive herself, she reasoned, how could God Almighty forgive her? This thought made me sad because she believed an accusatory voice. My heart broke for her. After I shared that truth in love, they departed. They vanished into thin air. The vision I was in was over as quickly as it had started. Did the three women accomplish what they set out to do? No! A resounding no since God's love overcomes fear.

I have no earthly idea how their story ended since I never saw the two other witches again. Maybe their story is still unfolding. I hope and pray that the conversational witch took the truth I shared with her about the Lord's love— namely His forgiveness— and asked God Almighty to forgive her for aborting her unborn child. Once forgiveness is received, I pray her life is forever changed by the author of love, Abba Father. In addition, I pray her surrendered life will lead many more witches to a loving relationship with Jesus Christ. My heart-felt desire is to one day meet her and her other two friends, either here on earth as believers or in heaven for eternity.

26

GOODBYE IS NEVER EASY

"Lord, how can I help my dad? He has helped
so many people over the course of his life.
Please, Lord, help me help my father."

In December 2008, my parents, Harry and Joan, were preparing to visit us for the holidays. What a treat! We were looking forward to celebrating Christ's birth with my parents, who raised me in God's beloved church. They were going to be our Christmas presents that year! Unfortunately, my mom and dad never made the trip. Plans changed quickly when my dad noticed a shortness of his breath while walking his beloved, English Setter. He ran some blood tests on himself and decided to schedule an appointment with the oncologists to confirm his self-diagnosis. A trip to Mayo Clinic in Rochester, Minnesota, confirmed it. At the age of 77, Harry, who otherwise was a picture of health, was diagnosed with acute myeloid leukemia. My dad had a decision to make. Fight the disease with chemotherapy or live the remainder of his time on this earth without that stress on his body. His doctors had given him three to six months to live.

I was absolutely devastated when I heard the news. My dad had always helped people achieve good health by helping them test for and understand their vitamin and mineral deficiencies. Of course, he also helped his patients with chiropractic treatment. He was my hero. He was honest, helpful, and caring. Instead of resting, he would use his Sunday afternoons to meet with his acute patients to give them the relief they desperately needed. I remember being a bit upset when hurting patients would get his attention after church instead of me. When I got wind of my dad's diagnosis and understood he would not be seeking modern medicine to treat and potentially heal his body, I began to pray. *"Lord, how can I help my dad? He has helped so many people throughout his life. Please, Lord, help me help my father."*

Afterward, it became clearer why the Lord may have brought us to Palm Beach County. Hippocrates Health Institute is in West Palm Beach. I spoke to my dad about attending the Institute to learn about a non-invasive way to help his body heal from this dis-ease. Initially, he was reluctant to a speak with the facility's head to understand what they could offer him. However, he finally agreed to listen and ask questions. Delighted, I scheduled the three-way phone call. The hour-long discussion took place and my father decided to come down and spend three weeks participating in their program. Dad agreed to be all in, to see if their approach could help his body heal itself given the right conditions. My mom came along with my dad for support, and they did the program together.

I will never forget picking them up at the airport and noticing my dad's jaundice-colored face and bloody gums, which are two obvious signs that his health was deteriorating quickly. I hid my concern, so he did not know what I observed. I cannot overstate how fervently I prayed for the sovereign Lord to restore my dad's health. I did not want to lose my daddy. I was scared.

My parents moved into their modest bedroom suite at Hippocrates. On the first day, the doctors ran my parents blood work to establish a baseline. They would compare the baseline to future blood work, to track improvements during the three-week intensive course. During my daily visits, I would join them for lunch. It took a very long time to eat because it required so much chewing. I referred to the meals—self-serve from an elaborate, health-conscious version of a salad bar—as rabbit food. However, I truly enjoyed the healthy salads and the sweet time with my parents. Harry and Joan were typically upbeat during this challenging health trial. They cracked jokes and helped others in the program to laugh and be at ease.

One young lady, who attended the same three weeks of training, stands out in my mind. She was angry and deeply depressed upon arrival. At the end of the stay, we gathered to learn about each person's progress. She shared that she had been addicted to sugar. It had controlled her life. She was now free from the addiction and had a positive outlook on her future. She was truly transformed emotionally and physically from the inside out. It was a huge blessing to witness her regain her health and mental outlook on life. Seeing her transformation, affirmed what my dad had always taught us. What we put in our mouths will significantly affect us positively or negatively. My mom was the next big winner. Initially, her cholesterol was in the high two hundreds, and it had dropped over a hundred points. Amazing!

My dad's skin color was back to normal, and his gums were no longer bleeding. He had an optimistic attitude. I do not remember the actual blood work results, but it, too, showed improvement. He had a new perspective about this disease and how he could battle it naturally. Later, he sent me a letter thanking me for saving his life. I know I did not save his life; God extended it to give us more time together.

My mom took on a mountain of work growing wheatgrass, sprouting seeds, and preparing food to keep my dad on the protocol they taught them. Unfortunately, she almost lost her life doing it. One day while picking up organic food from a grocery store about an hour's drive away, she ate something that harmed her. Thank the Lord! She survived the food poisoning and regained her energy after being cared for in the hospital for a week. During her stay, she received intravenous hydration replacing lost minerals and electrolytes.

The following year my dad was preparing to have my siblings and their families over to celebrate Christmas with them before he and my mom would head to Florida to celebrate with us. He chose to do what Hippocrates' health professionals had advised him not to do: stay away from harsh chemicals. Unfortunately, because of his desire to have the house look perfect for my siblings, he exposed himself to nasty chemicals while cleaning the kitchen cabinets. Consequently, it was shortly after that exposure that my siblings called and said, "Dad will not be coming to Florida." Upon hearing those words, my heart broke. It was time for me to visit him while he was still alive. I immediately packed my bags to catch a flight to my hometown.

During my stay, I helped my dad get their finances and paperwork in order. My visit was short, but productive. My young family needed me back home. A month later, I got the dreaded call that he was in the hospital and would most likely never return home. I hopped on the next flight to Chicago. From there, I drove to Sterling to say goodbye to my father before he took his last breath and joined his heavenly Father.

27

A LIE WORTH EXPOSING

"Lord, help me with this overwhelming grief!"

The night was bone-chilling cold when my beloved dad passed from this physical world into eternity on January 21, 2009. The entire family gathered in my hometown of Sterling, Illinois, to be with him in his final hours and to comfort him and each other. Mom and my oldest sister stayed at the hospital so Dad would not be alone. The pain was so great that the doctors ordered a self-controlled pump of morphine to be used at his discretion. When the pain was too intense, my dad would press the button and receive immediate relief. I had gone to my parents' home to rest. I was mentally and emotionally exhausted from seeing my amazing dad so weak and frail.

The phone rang. Those horrible yet somewhat relieving words were spoken, "Dad passed." Before the call came through, I knew he had taken his last breath. I distinctly remember sensing his spirit in the guest bedroom where I was staying. His sweet-tempered English Setter, Chelsea, had started to wag her tail. I believe she felt his presence in the bedroom as well. She missed him dearly while he was in the hospital. I was alarmed and concerned that I could sense his spirit. Consequently, I spoke out loud, "Dad, go to Jesus!" This sensing of him pretty much haunted me. Why did he visit Chelsea and me? Shouldn't he have gone directly to be with the Lord?

The next day we made all the necessary arrangements. My siblings, mother, and I made most of the decisions at the funeral home. We picked out a casket and reviewed the plans for the visitation and burial. The actual funeral was planned by my oldest siblings. I will never forget the frigid evening of his visitation. Many beloved people from our small town endured the freezing weather to pay their respects. They came to express their grief, their love, and their goodbyes to my father. These lovely people were lined up outside and around the building. He was truly respected and loved by many.

After returning home to our warm climate, waves of grief hit me. I could not endure the immense emotional pain. It was difficult to refer to my dad in the past tense. I was keeping him alive in my words but knowing well he had passed. I prayed, *"Lord, help me with this overwhelming grief!"* I shared this with my husband, and he supported me in seeking outside help. I reached out to Vickie Schleimer from CUMC. She shared with me a counseling ministry based on prayer and illuminating God's wisdom in trying circumstances. She sent me the names of two

Christian therapists trained in theophostic counseling in my area. I chose the woman therapist, Dr. Dolores Jacoby.

Working with Dr. Dolores saved my life and my marriage. She was an answer to my prayer. She helped me expose the lie that my dad was not with the Lord, which gave me the peace I needed. Let me explain the lie I believed. Because I sensed my dad's spirit at the house when he passed, I thought he had not gone to be with Jesus. The Holy Spirit-led counseling shed light onto the lies. Truth was ushered in, and the waves of grief stopped! This was a huge breakthrough for me.

Once I fully embraced the healing the Lord brought through prayerful grief counseling, Dr. Dolores asked if my husband was one hundred percent behind me. I said, "Yes," because he was the one who suggested that I get professional counseling. As a result, Dolores suggested that my husband and I began a program called *Prepare and Enrich* to enhance our marriage. We discussed it and decided to do it faithfully.

Investing in our relationship was well worth the time and energy. We know our strengths and our weaknesses. We learned the power of drive-through talking. To this day, we still have our weekly date nights. We escape for some quality time and adventure alone for long weekends. Dr. Dolores said, "You were one of my best clients because you took my recommendations and diligently applied them to your lives." With over thirty years of marriage under our belts, I love Andy more now than the day I married him. Truthfully, we still have our conflicts that require mutual effort to resolve. I do not believe there is a perfect marriage, one without any need of conflict resolution. Commitment takes work. I am working on loving him well.

28

HOME EDUCATION JOURNEY

*"Lord, if it is Your good and perfect will for me
to home educate, please give us unity."*
"Lord, which child should I home school?"
"You alone, Lord, be my recommendation."

I was elated to hear the words from one of my dear friends, Andrea, "You do not home educate your children unless God calls you to it." "Phew!" I exclaimed. I had escaped that daunting endeavor because He had not called me. I thought I had dodged that proverbial bullet. You may think that my thought process was a bit harsh, but I had no earthly idea how to educate my children at home! We were still living in a suburb of Houston, Texas, when Andrea imparted those words of wisdom. Looking back, I can honestly say that every year of home educating my children was a learning process.

The year the Lord called me to home educate is etched into my mind. It was a few years later when we moved to Wellington, where we had the joy of meeting many lovely people at Wellington Christian School (WCS). The school educated students from preschool through high school. Because we had packed up and moved to South Florida in late December, we had to enroll our kids into WCS in January. The school size alone was no comparison. Faith Lutheran School (FLS) had a few hundred families, while WCS had triple that number. It was a huge transition for our young children.

I loved our little Lutheran school in the suburbs of Houston. It was nothing to look at from the outside. However, the teachers loved the Lord, started the day with devotion, prayed for our young children, and imparted wisdom to them. FLS educated kids from kindergarten through eighth grade. Christiana was in third grade and had to leave her beloved teacher, Mrs. Thames. Luke was in kindergarten. In due time, they made the transition to WCS, and the following year Grace joined her older siblings.

While my kids were in school, I led women in Bible studies. In addition, one day a week, my hubby and I hosted and led a couples' evening Bible study. One of my beloved friends and her family came to the Lord through studying the Word with us. I will never forget asking Patricia repeatedly to check out our women's group. We were beginning to study *Believing God* by Beth Moore. One day, Patricia got tired of saying no. Ha! Ha! She jumped into the Bible study with both feet and the Lord wooed her into a loving relationship with Him. We began to pray for her husband, Dean. Not much later, he also accepted Jesus as his Lord and Savior. Her kids are still strong in the Lord today. What a blessing I received to witness an entire family's salvation. I share that story because Patricia is one of my friends who took the leap of faith to home educate our children together.

The conversation with Andy to discuss the possibility of home educating our children went something like this, "Honey, I keep running into people that are home educating their kids." His response, with much sass, went something like this, "What are you thinking?" My reaction to his sarcasm was short, "I do not know … I need to pray about it and investigate it some more." I prayed, *"Lord, if it is Your good and perfect will for me to home educate our kids, please give us unity."* Andy quickly said, "If you do this, how will our kids have friends and be social?" His concern seems to be a top apprehension for many parents considering the home education journey.

Based on my research, I quickly realized that a family could easily get overstimulated with all the extracurricular activities the home-educated kids could enjoy. For example, Saints, which is a physical education program, is offered half a day each week. Park days allowed the kids to play together one afternoon each month while the parents received encouragement from veteran homeschooling mothers. Teen groups met once a month to hang out and socialize. Weekly art classes and Girl Scouts were also fun activities. After church on Saturday evenings, our High Schoolers attended campfires with fun games and discipleship. The Parents Educating Children group offered many field trips that enhanced the students' educational experiences. We utilized these and other local home education opportunities to strengthen our kids' academic and social experiences. Add in our kids' sports, church, and youth group schedule—we were busy every day of the week and evenings.

My investigation took us to the largest U.S. Home Education Conference in Orlando, Florida. Some ten thousand participants attended that year. We have been attending every year since that first baptism by fire. I browsed through the largest vendor hall I had ever seen, including all the IBM events I once frequented. It took hours to peruse all the booths. An experienced home education mother told me not to buy anything at the convention. Instead, pray about each curriculum as I create a plan for each child. Wow! Given this vast candy store of educational wares from games to all-encompassing curriculums, how does one not buy anything?

I observed how respectful the young people attending the conference were to their parents and others. The kids' lovely behavior sold me. I wanted the same for my kids. Honestly, I already had respectful children. However, I wanted them to grow up loving the Lord their God with all their heart, mind, soul, and strength and loving one another. Teaching them at home would allow me to teach them the Word as part of their education. Maybe that is why God was putting this on my heart.

Upon returning home from Orlando, I spoke to my hubby and let him know I was seriously considering home educating our children even more now than before I left. He asked me to commit to having our kids tested every year to ensure they were getting taught what they needed for each grade level. Of course, I agreed. This was the unity I had asked God for.

Next, I prayed a simple prayer while I was rollerblading, *"Lord, which child should I home school?"* I honestly thought He was going to say my oldest. It seemed to make sense to me. I would figure out how to school the oldest, then add one kid at a time. Surprisingly, God was not thinking what I was thinking. I felt Him respond, "**I gave you all of them**." Woah! I hadn't signed up for that. Okay, now I was terrified! How do I home school all my children including our fifth, Caroline? My mind was baffled. I should have attended the breakout sessions at the conference that taught how to home educate many children. Regardless, God is so good, and He equips those He calls.

Little by little, year by year, He showed me how to teach those

He entrusted into my care. I was not the perfect home educator. However, with the help of outside resources, the kids tested well. When it came time for my oldest to enter high school, I was baffled again. So, I researched how to home educate through high school. A friend "just happened" to mention an opportunity for my oldest called Home Education Enrichment Day (HEED), and she told me to look at the website called takeheed.org. HEED is a home education program for middle schoolers and high schoolers to prepare them for college. The program looked great. The only problem was that I needed two letters of recommendation to be considered. I told my mom about the opportunity. Since I knew no one in Boca Raton, as we drove down the road, we prayed, *"You alone, Lord, be my recommendation."* Boca, as we call it, is located 45 minutes southeast of our home in Wellington. Overwhelming gratefulness does not begin to describe how I felt toward the Lord when I received a call back for an interview. It was obvious; He opened the door. All five kids attended this incredible college preparatory program. Sue Puchferran, one of the three directors, became a dear friend of mine. She kindly referred to me as her "stalker" because I would attend all her presentations and pay close attention to her every word. I even took detailed notes. I learned so much from her "How to Home School Through High School" presentations. She had more knowledge in her little pinky than anyone else I knew. I needed that knowledge, and she was happy to share it with me and anyone that wanted to learn.

At HEED, my children attended classes taught by professional teachers one day a week. The teachers impart the weeks' worth of material in 80-minute classes. The classes are small to reinforce an excellent student-to-teacher ratio. They expanded to elementary-age kids. During Covid-19 pandemic, HEED launched an online program to accommodate families home education needs. God positioned them perfectly to handle the worldwide health crisis without missing a beat.

We stayed the course, home educating our kids for twelve

and a half years, until we moved a bit too far from Boca. Our move happened before they launched the online version of HEED. I am prayerful HEED will continue to be a blessing to the home school community as well as those just jumping into the home education adventure.

29

FIREWORKS

"Lord, please keep my babies safe. Help them to love You with all their heart, mind, soul, and strength. Let them dream of Your heavenly kingdom and how they can be used for Your glory. Amen."

O n the afternoon of May 10, my boys were playing basketball in our neighbor's driveway. Upon chasing a ball into the bushes, they noticed an outside pipe leaking a significant amount of water. My kids attempted to duct tape the pipe to stop the leak, to no avail. When they told me about it, I immediately called our neighbor, Derek, to let him know about the leak and see if we could help. Before hanging up the phone, we discussed the lack of an offer for his house which was for sale. He shared with me that he had just decided to take it off the market in hopes of getting a long-term rental, while waiting for the housing market to rebound. Derek and Peng bought their outdated home at the height of the housing market and wanted to sell the house for what he had paid for it. My heart went out to him, and I wanted to help. I let Derek know I would get the word out to my homeschool group, sports teams, and our church. I commented, "Who knows? Maybe it will be a blessing to someone we know."

—

Unsettled feelings overcame my body every time I passed through my home's narrow hallway from the dining room to the kitchen. I strolled by the air conditioner return vent many times throughout the day since this was the path from my bedroom to the kitchen. The other side of the return air duct was the electrical panel to our house, which was inside the attached three-car garage. I had this nagging feeling that something was just not right. However, I could never put my finger on it. Words cannot explain the bothersome sense I felt each time I walked through that hallway. I prayed multiple times, especially at night, when the eerie sensation seemed the strongest. A semi-retired pastor from our church came to the house and prayed through the entire house with me. Maybe that is how I finally gained a sense of peace in that hallway. It was disturbing, but eventually I was able to keep it from bothering me. Peace is something that we need to receive from the Lord daily. I have heard it said that peace is fleeting. I am thankful that God's presence is not fleeting. Instead, it transcends all understanding.

As the day May 10, 2010, came to an end, I put our two youngest girls, Grace (8) and Caroline (3), to bed. I fell asleep at the end of their bed. Before we fell asleep, I prayed, *"Lord, please keep my babies safe. Help them to love You with all their heart, mind, soul, and strength. Let them dream of Your heavenly kingdom and how they can be used for Your glory. Amen."*

Before I knew it, I, too, had fallen into a deep asleep. Suddenly, I was awakened by the sound of loud fireworks. Since it was not the Fourth of July nor New Year's Eve, I struggled to make sense of the fireworks. Given my level of exhaustion, I quickly fell back asleep. A few minutes later, I heard loud and glorious sounds of rockets exploding in the air. This time, it startled me into awareness of my surroundings. I thought, *what in the world was making these misplaced noises?* Staggering out of my girls' bedroom and down the stairs, I noticed the kitchen clock at 11:45 p.m. Next, I opened the door to the garage to see my husband's workbench light lit. Hmm? I was too tired to walk into the garage to turn it off. Choosing to leave it on, I shut and locked the garage door. Half asleep, I walked down the hallway, the one I described earlier, and I found my way through the dark to my bedroom. I threw on my PJs and removed my contacts. Finally, I snuggled into the comfort of my bed. Andy barely noticed my presence, as he continued to snore obnoxiously while I quickly drifted off to sleep.

Fifteen minutes later, the rude awakening of our smoke detector blaring in my ears hit me hard! My hubby, who can sleep through anything, continued to sleep until I whacked him with my hand squarely on his chest. "What is going on?" he abruptly inquired. I yelled to be heard over the deafening alarm, "The fire alarm is going off! How can this be?" Andy reminded me that he had just changed all the batteries on the alarms, so it was not caused by a failing battery. It must be a real fire alarm! I jumped to my feet, half-blind, in the dark, and ran to the kitchen. By this time, Luke, our oldest son at eleven years old, screamed, "Mom, it's a fire. Smoke is billowing up the stairs!" I yelled to Andy, "Call 911; we have a fire!" I followed the smoke to the garage door and felt the solid wood fire door. The high heat that came off the door handle made it too hot to touch. Andy ran up the steps to grab our youngest, Caroline. Christiana, our oldest at age thirteen, had already brought Caroline to the top of the stairs. Andy grabbed Caroline and headed down the steps. Then, Christiana woke Grace as Luke woke Josh to head down the stairs to the front door. I stood in the entryway looking down the hallway and noticed the lights flicker while counting my kids as they scurried out the front door. To our surprise, Christiana went back to her room to grab her puppy dog, Jake. She was the last child to leave our burning home.

We ran across the street and pounded on our neighbor's door to let us into their home! Dave thought we were intruders. Once he realized it was us, he opened his door, and we filed into their living room. Before we knew it, eighteen fire vehicles lined our street, and the fire fighters labored to put out the blazing fire. We huddled together on Dave's couch and prayed for the safety of the firefighters while they risked their lives to put out the raging fire and save our beloved pets. Not one firefighter was injured. One strong firefighter walked out of our burning house carrying my daughter's 20-gallon turtle tank. I am not kidding! Ms. Lucky, our beloved Canadian scaredy-cat, went missing for a few days and turned up after we left food out for her. Another firefighter brought out our other frisky feline safe and sound. He said her eyes lit up from the flashlights. Amazingly, she stayed on the kitchen counter, awaiting her rescuers. She was probably scared stiff.

Life and death hung in the balance of a matter of seconds. The fire chief told me we had approximately 40 seconds to get out of our home. Had we not gotten out when we did, the kids upstairs would have died from smoke inhalation. To this day, that thought sends unnerving feelings through my body and mind. Then I am reminded and grateful that God Almighty answered my simple prayer and protected our babies that ominous night.

In addition, I am grateful for the conversation with Derek just seven hours prior to the fire. The Lord knew what we needed before we knew it. The yellow warning tape strung across the front pillars made it evident that our home was condemned. Now homeless, we would need a new place to call home. God's timing is perfect. The Lord provided Derek's house, which was so convenient for us to move into. Not only was God's timing perfect, but His provision was spot on! We were the ones who would be renting our next-door neighbor's home. Our family was safe and sound. That was enough of a blessing. Looking back, I saw God's hand protect, and move us forward from this tragedy. God is so good and faithful!

30

YOU WILL BE WELL AGAIN

"Lord, should I go to the ER, and if so, which one?"
"Lord, help me."

A stage IV Lymphoma diagnosis, because there is no stage III, is not what anyone wants to hear. After five long days of being poked, prodded, and cut open at JFK Hospital in West Palm Beach, FL, the outcome was a dreadful diagnosis. The team of doctors assigned to my case included: an infectious disease specialist, a hematologist oncologist, and a general MD. Let me tell the entire story, because it has an inspiring ending fueled by a simple prayer.

In November of 2012, one of our beloved cats went missing. As all good pet parents do, we posted a photo of her on all the stop signs in our neighborhood, along with a message that she was missing. An older gentleman called and said he had not seen our cat, but he had some kittens recently born in his backyard. He wanted to know if we would be interested in one of them. We talked it over and decided to look at them.

How could we resist a cute little kitten the size of my two hands cupped together that had been orphaned and needed some care? We only had it a few days before heading to Orlando for a Thanksgiving soccer tournament. We could not leave it home alone, so we decided to take it with us. The long weekend came to an end, but I began having lower back pain on the trip home. It felt like my lovely monthly cycle with pain radiating from my lower back. Luckily, Andy was kind enough to drive the entire way home. I took it easy for the next few days and started to feel better. A week or so later, the same thing happened again. I noticed that I would get flu-like symptoms with body aches that radiated from my lower back. I would rest for a couple of days and then regain my strength. The struggle to stay well continued. With each bout of the illness, I noticed my stomach becoming enlarged. It was so strange.

Andy, knowing how much I love cycling, bought me a bicycle to replace the one destroyed in the fire. He wanted to help me start exercising again, thinking that would help me regain my health. We found a used Specialized road bike in Tampa to fit my small stature. He flew me there to give it a whirl and I fell in love with it. After purchasing it, we dropped it off at a bicycle shop to ship it to our house. I proceeded to the airport to catch a quick flight home. On the way home, I started to feel horrible all over again. This battle for healthy days was frustrating and had started to concern me.

About five weeks after we adopted our feral kitten, I finally made an appointment to see my family doctor. It was a Friday, and they got me in right away for an appointment. Dr. Apicella was unavailable. As a result, I saw his physician's assistant. After a lot of questions, my illness was still a mystery. I let her know that we took in a feral kitten, and it had scratched me. I mentioned that I was not too concerned because I was not pregnant. I also shared with her that we lived on a large property and the back yard was very wooded. We treated the property for pests, and we had found Cain frogs with enlarged ticks on their backs. She ordered an immediate CT scan. Before I left the office she said, "I am going to prescribe some antibiotics. If you get worse over the weekend, go to the emergency room."

Off I went to have a CT scan. The process was painless. However, it took a while since they were working me into their busy Friday afternoon schedule. I knew I was not going to be able to get the official results soon since it was already the end of the week. Therefore, I decided to ask the radiologist what he saw. He was kind enough to tell me that he did not know what was causing my lymph nodes to be so swollen. But he did note that they were the size of grapes! I left with more concern and feeling extremely exhausted. I headed home for some much-needed rest.

Saturday came and went. I did not leave my bed that day except to use the restroom. The next morning, Andy, being super-dad, was busy with our kids while I was home resting. I was having trouble reading, so I made my way to my bathroom to locate a fresh pair of contacts. Unfortunately, I was completely out and needed my old prescription filled. I reached out to two of my besties for help. Dr. Dolores Jacoby and Patricia Anthony drove to Costco for me, and then they stopped by to drop off my contacts. Upon entering my master bedroom, my dear friends were immediately alarmed. They checked my temperature and asked me how I was feeling. I let them know that I felt horrible. I had a low-grade fever and my stomach looked as though I was seven months pregnant. My friends told me they thought I needed to go to the ER. What did we do next? Yes, we prayed, *"Lord, should I go to the ER, and if so, which one?"*

My friends called Andy. They told him how concerned they were, and that they planned to take me to JFK Hospital immediately. He appreciated the help, given his hands were full taking care of our five kids. Off I went. I grabbed the CT scan disc, taken two days prior, so that the doctors could evaluate the film. At that point, all I knew was that I had swollen lymph nodes the size of grapes. If that information is not sound alarming, it should. Our lymph nodes should not be the size of grapes, let alone peas. The lymphatic system is the drainage system that rids our body of harmful pathogens. My lymphatic system was clogged up. But by what?

The handsome, young admitting doctor told me I was sick with either one of two things: cancer or an infectious disease. He asked, "On a scale of one to ten—ten being the highest—what is your current level of pain?" I answered, "Seven or eight." Next, he asked about my pain tolerance. I told him it was high, built up after having birthed five babies. Finally, he asked if I had ever had morphine. I said emphatically, "No, and I do not want any." After further examining my abdomen, he stated, "I am ordering it for you." That upset me because I did not want to be under the influence of anything that would not allow me to know what was happening to my body. At the same time, I felt I was under his care and needed him to make that decision. By this time, Dolores had joined me in the ER. She saw them administer the drug. She also saw the tears in my eyes as the morphine slowly relaxed my body.

Next, the admitting doctor ordered another CT scan. I had given him the SCSI drive with the images from Friday's CT scan, but the images were the size of a thumbnail. Those images were not going to help the ER doctors. They wheeled me to the imaging room. They told me what to expect and had me lay face up. As I lay on the table, waiting for further instructions, I was praying, *"Lord, help me."* I heard a response in my head that said, **"You will get well again, but it is going to take time."** Those perfectly timed words I heard from the Lord gave me much relief! Now, I had what I needed to stand firm no matter which diagnosis I had to face. Because I knew His voice and knew I heard clearly from Him, His words brought me much peace.

Peace is what I needed, especially with the shared room I found myself in. Each day, my new roommates would arrive and then depart. For some strange reason, they had me on a floor that turned people around quickly. Boy, I wanted to be one of those people going home the next day. Unfortunately, that wasn't my experience. While I was there, the hospital team poked, prodded, drew blood, extracted lymph nodes, and even administered a spinal tap. Indeed, I felt they would be able to figure out what was wrong with me. Either way, I knew I would be well again, but it was going to take time.

By the end of the week, Andy brought our oldest son, Luke, to visit. At the time, he was only fourteen years old. In fact, the timing of his visit was not good. Right before they arrived, the hematologist oncologist walked into my room to give me some disturbing news. Dr. C. entered the room with a serious look on his face. He quickly blurted out that the infectious disease doctor had found nothing to cause the swelling of my lymph nodes. He declared, "It must be cancer. Stage IV Lymphoma because there is no Stage III. Now, we need to find where it is coming from." He continued to explain that there was no reason to keep me in the hospital. He said, "Go home and await the results from the spinal tap and the lymph node biopsy." He added, "Schedule a follow-up at my office for two weeks from now."

The first meeting at my hematologist oncologist's office was disappointing. He explained that he no idea where the cancer was coming from, but he was sure that it was causing the swelling because the infectious disease doctor found nothing. He gave me marching orders to start meeting with all the specialists that could potentially identify the origin of the cancer.

My friends had become very concerned. They brought meals to our house while I was in the hospital and upon my return home. I tried to update my friends who were not living in our proximity by making Facebook posts. I had many appointments with multiple doctors trying to figure out the source of the cancer. The abdomen specialist said, "You do not look like you have cancer, and I see a lot of patients with cancer." His words were the first bit of good news. Also, he stated he would do more damage by opening my abdomen trying to find the cancer and then attempting to extract it. Thank goodness surgery was out of the question. After a few more doctor visits under my belt, I finally got to see a familiar face in one of the white coats.

One of my doctor appointments was with my gynecologist and soccer mom friend, Dr. Graham-Brown. She asked a lot of questions. One had to do with my eyesight. I remembered my girlfriends had brought me my contacts to help me with my vision. *Hmm,* I thought to myself, *maybe I needed to see my optometrist, Dr. Abdal.* In addition, Dr. Graham-Brown shared valuable advice that stuck with me. She said, "Karen, you are smart. You need to be your own healthcare advocate."

Given those words of encouragement, I made an appointment right away to see Dr. Abdal. She worked me into her schedule the same day. Dr. Abdal was shocked when she looked into my eyes. Then she used her specialized equipment to take pictures of my eyes. What startled her the most was that she could not see the optic nerve. She showed me the electronic images taken before my illness. They were dramatically different from the ones taken that afternoon. Immediately, she called a friend, an ophthalmologist, to get me in to see him the following day. I had shared all this information with my friend, Dr. Dolores. She had been diagnosed with eye cancer and knew all the best eye doctors in the area. She got me an appointment to see Dr. May, a neuro ophthalmologist in Boca Raton. Thankfully, they put me on the calendar for the following afternoon.

A new day dawned, and I was optimistic! When the

ophthalmologist, who Dr. Abdal referred me to, looked into my eyes, his expression changed dramatically. He looked like he had seen a ghost! Attempting to comfort him, I quickly explained that I had heard a voice going into the second CT scan. And it told me that I would be well again, but it would take time. I was adamant—I was sure it was the Lord's voice. The information I shared seemed to give him a tiny amount of relief, but he did not gain the same peace that I had received. Immediately, he said, "You need to see a neuro ophthalmologist." I let him know I already had an appointment scheduled with Dr. May. He said, "Perfect. He is the best!" He sent word to Dr. May that I would be coming to see him.

The drive to Boca was nothing unusual. At this point, Dr. May was one of the many doctors I had seen to help determine the origin of the cancer. I am a firm believer that finding the root cause of a health issue is the beginning of the healing process. Andy had been a gem taking me to doctor appointment after doctor appointment. We were hopeful this doctor might be able to figure out what was going on inside of me.

After checking in with the receptionist, we sat patiently in the waiting room. Andy had removed himself to take a business-related phone call. His boss, Jason Judge, had been super supportive and told him to take as much time as needed to help me. During his phone call, they called me back to the examining room. They placed my forehead to rest on an oddly shaped machine. Inside, red dots appeared in the image of a cross. Sound odd? Maybe so, but that is what I saw. There were two lines of red dots, one vertical and one horizontal, intersecting in the middle of the screen, making perfect right angles. It was the shape of a cross!

Next, Dr. May stepped into the room and introduced himself. Before I knew it, he was looking into my eyes. There was no time to explain what I had repeated over and over to each physician: "We took in a feral kitten. It scratched me. However, I was not concerned because I was not pregnant." Toxoplasmosis is concerning if one is pregnant. This infection can be transferred from cats to humans by the animal's feces. The symptoms were similar, but again: I was not pregnant. I also told the many doctors I had seen over the course of this illness that we lived on over an acre of property—plenty of woodsy area where ticks thrive.

My hubby was still outside taking his call when Dr. May made an interesting sound as though he was intrigued. I quickly inquired, "What do you see?" "Hmm," was his response. "Let me keep looking." After checking the other eye, he suggested he knew what was ailing me. "Really?" I excitedly probed. Could this finally be the answer? I thought to myself. Could this be the beginning of my healing? About that time, Andy walked into the examining room. The brilliant doctor calmly explained, "This is a rare disease. I see about one case per year. Have you been around any cats lately? Specifically, kittens? Because with this infection they do not survive to adulthood." I was shocked! How in the world did he know we had taken in a feral kitten? Dr. May was the first doctor who did not have that necessary piece of the puzzle. My husband, coming in a bit late to the examination, thought I had told the good doctor.

Immediately, I explained to Andy that I did not have a chance to tell Dr. May about our feral kitten nor about living on one and a quarter acre. Dr. May beat me to the punch. He declared, "I believe you have Bartonella disease." It did not ring a bell. He continued, "Are you familiar with the song, "Cat Scratch Fever?" Andy questioned, "The one by Ted Nugent?" Dr. May responded, "Yes, it refers to this disease. I will have to run some blood tests to confirm my clinical diagnosis." We were elated! If he was correct, I was on the road to healing.

While waiting for my test results, we had another appointment with Dr. Mitch Ghen. Our meeting with him was quick. He looked at my lab work, and we told him my story. He said very frankly, "If you have cancer, I cannot help you. However, if you have an infectious disease, I can help you get well." Convinced that Dr. May had figured it out, I could not wait any longer. I needed to start treatment right away. I was not living at that point; I was surviving, laying around like a lazy, fat cat. In fact, in a desperate attempt to get me moving, Andy moved my new Specialized road bike into my bedroom and placed it on a stationary wheel to give me incentive to get back on it and ride. Unfortunately, I had no energy, regardless of my desire. Because of my enlarged abdomen and swollen lymph nodes, clothes did not fit. Exhaustion had the best of me. Eating was not a pleasure since foods made my stomach extend even further. I wondered when relief was to come.

We discussed Dr. Mitch Ghen's protocol some more. I convinced Andy that I needed to take this calculated risk and start the protocol since Dr. Mitch was an expert on medical-grade silver treatments. We agreed I would proceed without receiving the official results from the blood work ordered by Dr. May. We further discussed the cost of the treatment. It was not cheap. And insurance would not cover it. Equally important, we discussed the logistics of getting me to Boca three times a week for treatments. The intravenous (IV) infusions would take three to five hours, depending on how my body reacted to the silver. I was ready for treatment, healing, and going through what was necessary to regain my health. My hubby was reluctant since the treatment was not mainstream protocol.

In the interim, my blood work came back positive for Bartonella disease. I was referred to an infectious disease doctor at Palms West Hospital, about a mile from our house. I went to visit him. He laid out the potential protocol: three to six months on IV antibiotics. He said they did not have any data that this antibiotic protocol would work because Bartonella disease is so rare. However, he was hopeful it would help. My body never responded well to antibiotics. I knew in my heart that my body could not stand three to six months of antibiotics. I tried to politely decline the treatment, telling the good doctor that I appreciated his time and honesty. I let him know that I would prayerfully consider the antibiotic protocol, however, I highly doubted I would proceed with his suggested course of action.

Joan, my beloved mother, at seventy-seven years young, volunteered to drive me to and from Boca. In addition, she committed to sit with me as I endured the needle and the IV drip that stung the area of my arm where I was poked two times a week, allowing the Argentyn23 Silver to flow through my veins. The third visit included a high dose of vitamin C and other immune-boosting vitamins and minerals administered through an IV. The proposed duration of the treatment was three weeks. Two weeks into the treatment, I began to feel better. My energy slowly returned. My immune system started to kick in, and I began to regain my life. I respectfully told Dr. Mitch, which he preferred to be called, that I felt I had enough of the treatment. My veins near the pokes had hardened somewhat from the silver. My body was doing what it was supposed to do: fight the infection. Dr. Mitch kindly accepted my decision, and I stayed on the oral doses for another week or so.

I will never forget that spring, specifically our first family trip together since becoming deathly ill. We visited the capital of Florida, Tallahassee, for a home-education day with the legislators, and then we went off to swim with the manatees in the estuary the next day. How much fun to have a life again—and have it abundantly. All those faithful prayers for my health were answered. God is so good. I was now well, and it did take time.

31

FIVE STEPS TO RESTORE YOUR HEALTH

"Lord, please help my daughter."
*"Lord, I have tried so many protocols to heal
me and my kids. I am sorry I didn't come to You
first. I am at my wit's end. Please, help me!"*

You may believe one mysterious disease in a lifetime is enough. I agree. It seems I passed the first health trial with flying colors. Only once did I lose my composure during the lymphoma misdiagnosis. After talking to my brother, Dr. Tom, about the complications of lymphoma, the fear that struck me produced a gut reaction of dry heaves. My husband became scared and took me to the hospital. This unnecessary trip to the hospital was very early on in the entire ordeal. In hindsight, the biggest mistake I made was losing sight of what the Lord told me, **"You will be well again, but it is going to take time."**

After regaining my health, I took a good look at the two-inch-thick documentation on me from JFK Hospital. The doctors and nurses had observed my emotional health. They had taken notes and documented it. Each notation stated that I was in good spirits. How could I not be when I knew I had heard from the Lord a good prognosis? I did not fear what I had to walk through because I knew I would be well again. I prayed over and over, and the Lord opened the doors for me, which is how I ended up at Dr. Mitch Ghen's office. Unfortunately, this next health story is quite different.

It all started when my oldest daughter went to the University of Florida for her first year of college. She was ready for college and planned to live with one of her friends as her roommate. Her future looked bright. However, I started to receive concerning calls from her. On the first phone call, she said, "Mom, I cannot get up for my morning classes." I went into problem-solving mode. My first inquiry was related to her sleep cycle, "What time are you going to bed?" "Normal time," she replied. I had no reason not to believe her. The next time she called, she told me she had fallen, for no apparent reason, while going down the library steps. Hmm, I had no explanation to even begin to apply to that concern. The subsequent calls were more alarming. "Mom, I am having a horrible migraine." I replied, "Go to sleep. You will feel better in the morning." The next day she called to explain that she still felt horrible, as though a Mack truck had hit her. The symptoms did not compute. The few migraines I had in years past were always gone by the following day. The next call concerned me the most. "Mom, I had a seizure before this migraine started!" My immediate response was, "How quickly can you get home?" My thought was to drive the five hours to Gainesville, Florida to pick her up and bring her home. However, my dear friend, Patricia Anthony, was already in Orlando that day, which was a little more than halfway to Gainesville. If Christiana's friends could get her to Orlando, Patricia would bring her home. I said a simple prayer, *"Lord, please help my daughter."*

She made it home safely, and then the many doctor visits commenced. We were chasing another mystery disease that was harming my beloved firstborn. I wondered; how could this be happening? What was going on? Our primary caregiver, Dr. Apicella, did his best to figure it out and sent us to multiple specialists. The neurologist ruled out epilepsy which causes seizures. He had her do an MRI with a heavy-metal-based contrast called Gadolinium-Based Contrast Agents. It turns out that the heavy metal used, gadolinium, caused another strange symptom to appear later. It caused swollen and frozen joints in her finger and toes. After the fact, we found out that studies show people of Northern European descent have a high probability of not being able to naturally remove gadolinium from their bodies. This unfortunate situation made me so upset. By trying to help Christiana, we only made things worse. Had we known in advance, we might have made a different decision. Lesson learned. Pray first and ask lots of questions!

All the tests from multiple doctors were coming back negative. Christiana slept during the day and was awake at night. She had no energy all day long. At night, Sanna (Christiana's nickname) laid in her bed exhausted but awake, wondering when the next debilitating complex migraine would hit. These are just a few of the odd symptoms she experienced. The worst part was that many of the doctors were chalking up all these symptoms to something in her head. Even some people in my family were calling her symptoms psychosomatic, which added to the emotional pain she was experiencing.

I could see Sanna was struggling. She stayed home for the spring semester and attempted a few online courses from her university. She could not think straight enough to write a simple business letter. I knew the severity of her illness when she asked me to help with a writing assignment. The assignment was to write a letter explaining her disappointment with a make-believe product, but she had no idea how to start or finish the simple letter. Did she lose confidence in her writing ability? Or could she not mentally process the assignment? From that day forward, I knew Christiana was seriously ill because she had always been an excellent writer.

After meetings with a dozen or so doctors without a confirmed diagnosis, it was time to see Dr. Mitch Ghen. He had helped me with my mystery disease. Maybe he could help diagnose Christiana and help restore her health. We met with Dr. Mitch, and right away she was given hope. He told her he could help her. In my mind, it was not much of a gamble since the Lord had used Dr. Mitch to get me healthy. However, we still did not have a firm diagnosis for her symptoms. She signed up to have a pick line put in her arm, with a small tube running the Argentyn23 silver directly to her heart. Her heart would then pump the silver through her entire system. She was a brave young woman at the age of eighteen.

A week into the treatments, she experienced a frightening episode. She started to feel horrible: losing her balance, having immense pain, all the while not knowing what was causing this intense reaction. I was not home when it happened. The reaction subsided, and she told me about it when I returned home. I said, "Let's tell Dr. Mitch at your next visit to see what he thinks could have caused it." I will never forget that day in his office. He had a visiting doctor that asked a few questions. He was similar in age to Dr. Mitch and somewhat quiet. He listened to what we had to say, and then he said, "What you described sounded like a Jarisch-Herxheimer reaction." I thought, a WHAT reaction? Dr. Mitch discounted the comment by his peer, but, for whatever reason, it stuck in my head. I went home and told a friend, Tonya, what the visiting doctor had mentioned. Tonya had some of her own strange symptoms which kept reappearing. She was trying to figure out what was causing her skin to break out in hives. We talked, and she explained what she knew about Jarisch-Herxheimer reaction. She described it as the body reacting to many toxins dying off, in turn making one feel horrible. The die-off is typically related to Borrelia burgdorferi bacteria, otherwise known as Lyme disease.

Finally, we had a clue as to what was happening to my brave daughter. I reached out to one of my sisters because her oldest daughter had Lyme disease in high school and got over it. She told me about Dr. Zang in New York City. I quickly ordered his book and read it front to back. I called to schedule a phone consult. We sent blood work and scheduled a call to Dr. Zang. He clinically diagnosed Sanna over the phone with Lyme disease, based on her litany of symptoms, and suggested she start his protocol.

We shared this new information with Dr. Mitch, but he was not 100% on board with this diagnosis. He thought Sanna needed a small dose of hormones to help regain her energy. I spoke to my brother, Dr. Tom, about what Dr. Mitch prescribed. He said it took him years to help some patients get off very low doses of what Dr. Mitch suggested. We took the prescription, but she never took the hormones. However, Christiana continued receiving the Argengyn23 silver IVs, and she began taking Dr. Zang's supplement-based protocol. Christiana started to come back to life about three weeks into the IV protocol and one week into Dr. Zang's protocol! Her immune system began to pick up. We were looking forward to my niece's wedding at the end of April. Christiana was well enough to attend, and she looked beautiful!

—

I wish the Lyme story ended there. Unfortunately, it did not. Luke got sick for about two weeks with flu-like symptoms during his junior year of high school. He rarely got sick, and if he did, it was for just a few days. It was very odd that Luke could not shake the illness quickly. In addition, during the football season that same year, he suffered a painful infection in his mouth. Luckily, one of his football coaches, Dr. Mauk, happened to be an oral surgeon. He knew exactly what to do for the infection. He prescribed an oral medication that cleared up the infection. These peculiar yet small health trials stuck in my mind. When it was time for summer football training to start, Luke needed a new physical. I asked the doctor to run the titer for Lyme disease. At first, he brushed off my request. After I had laboriously explained that our oldest daughter was in the process of getting well from Lyme disease, the doctor consented. The test came back positive. Now, it was time to run the Western Blot test for Lyme disease and its common co-infections for the entire the family. We all took the tests prior to leaving for a youth mission trip to Belle Glade, Florida.

With the testing behind us, our oldest kids and I were off to Belle Glade to serve in the community. The trip to Belle Glade was my kids' favorite mission trip. They all served every year; from the time they started in middle school through high school graduation. This particular year, I volunteered as a life group leader for our middle school girls. Luke was already there serving when his test results came back positive for Lyme and one co-infection. Unfortunately, each one of us had positive Lyme bands, except for Andy. Thankfully, we did not have any of the horrible symptoms Christiana had suffered for well over a year. However, we still needed to address this serious disease. My heart broke. I had already witnessed Christiana battle her way back from this dreadful systemic infection. Now, all my kids and I had to fight for our lives. I do not want to sound dramatic, but the number one cause of death from Lyme disease is suicide. Many Lyme patients suffer for a very long time, both physically and mentally, until they give up and take their own lives. It's a horrible disease!

As soon as we got home from the mission trip, it was time to leave again on a much-anticipated vacation to Alaska. Going away at that time was the last thing I wanted to do, knowing the battle we faced. The youngest four children and I started Dr. Zang's protocol. The kids quickly rejected the allicin pills that made us all stink like garlic from every sweat gland in our bodies. Dr. Zang had another option, but it was not strong enough. After five months of the six-month protocol, only one child was healthy.

In addition to Dr. Zang's protocol, our primary health care provider, Dr. Apicella, gave us two weeks of antibiotics which made the mild symptoms even more prevalent. He warned us before taking them that it could worsen our symptoms since we did not know when we were infected. I did not pray. We rolled the dice and started the doxycycline. Unfortunately, our doctor's warning was spot on. We got worse. Doxy is the antibiotic that works, assuming the doctors accurately diagnose the disease right away. Given our adverse reaction, we probably had Lyme for much longer than two weeks. This disease was slowly invading our systems. When our bodies became stressed, as it did for Luke during football season, it would rear its ugly head in some form of an infection. Grace's overwhelming symptom was throwing up when she was stressed. She would be playing on the soccer field and throwing up on the sidelines. After her stomach was empty of whatever was in it, she was fine and would play at an exceptional level. Josh responded favorably to Dr. Zang's protocol. Our fifth and youngest child, Caroline, suffered from constant tummy and head pain. She responded well to the subsequent and major IV treatment. Unfortunately, that was not the case for the rest of us.

One failed treatment would lead to another failed treatment. We spent hours upon hours and an excessive amount of money trying to regain my family's health. Insurance covers antibiotics and blood work but nothing else. It's a costly disease to contract, and it was harming all my babies. A woman can never truly understand a mother's love until she becomes a mom. Instead of holding fast to my faith, I worked hard to find a cure for my kids and myself. While frantically searching for a cure, fear had replaced my faith.

—

We searched for a "Lyme-literate" doctor. Unfortunately, the closest one we could find was a two-hour drive from our home. As a result, the four of us began the trek to Vero Beach three times a week to receive phosphatidylcholine IVs. During one of our many visits, I will never forget what the nurturing nurse said to us, "You need to be grounded." At the time, I had no idea what she meant. I researched grounding and came up with grounding blankets. No kidding, I bought two of them: one for me and for my child who was interested in trying it. I should have known the 'grounding' that I needed comes from having a strong relationship with our creator, God Almighty. The four weeks of IVs seemed to work wonders until hurricane Matthew struck. With the low-pressure system bearing down on us, plus the physical preparation to secure our home, once again our health began to deteriorate. Knowing how much God loves my children and me, and how He miraculously healed and directed me to the cure for Bartonella disease, I reasoned that He could heal us this time as well. I prayed, *"Lord, I have tried so many protocols to heal my kids and me. I am sorry I didn't come to You first. I am at my wit's end. Please, help me!"*

After that prayer, He led me to Dr. Jay Davidson, the author of *5 Steps to Restoring Health Protocol*. I read his book from front to back, marked it up, and underlined it. It made complete sense to me. His wife almost died because of Lyme disease. As a result, Dr. Jay gave up his chiropractic practice to help her. In his book, he shares what he learned by trial and error.

During my next consultation with the "Lyme-literate" doctor in Vero Beach, I shared everything I learned from the book.

Unfortunately, we paid thousands of dollars to her to help get us well. Her protocols had helped, but when our bodies became stressed, we began to suffer all over again. She agreed with everything I shared with her regarding Dr. Jay's book. I got busy praying about which simple step I should take from his book. I would try one treatment for a week or so and note any changes in my health. Then I would pray again as to which protocol to try next. At this point, I was focusing on myself, hoping to transfer gained knowledge to my three oldest children. I had no problem being the guinea pig to help them. In fact, I preferred it.

Over the next few months, I began to regain my energy. I even went to Epcot with my husband and our two youngest children who, I might add, had received relief of their symptoms. One of their best friends came with us too. This outing was the first trip away from home in at least six months. It was so good to be out and about, having fun with some of my family, even though I was not completely well. After much prayer, my hubby and I decided Dr. Jay was the doctor we should work with as we focused on our family's health journey.

It was the end of December when we reached out to Dr. Jay, sent lab work, and scheduled our first call. The doctor asked an excellent question, "What part of your health do you want restored first?" My immediate response was my brain. I had no short-term memory, and my thought process was slow at best. In addition, my husband wanted my energy restored.

As the call was wrapping up, Dr. Jay commented, "Since you are not on death's doorstep, you are not a candidate for my services." Dr. Jay Davidson truly wanted to help those who had no hope, and I had hope. I knew what I had tried from his book was working, and I just needed more help. Dr. Jay gave me an excellent referral to one of the doctors who was part of his team, Dr. Nicholas Ellenson. Dr. Nick was fantastic! We talked once a month, and he coached me on restoring my health which, in turn, assisted me with restoring my children's health. My kids were at different points in their healing. They were willing to try some but not all of Dr. Jay's and Dr. Nick's protocols. I empathized with their position. They are much younger than I and, therefore, typically heal much faster. Dr. Jay Davidson truly wanted to help those who had no hope, and I had hope.

I remember my first call with Dr. Nick in January of 2017. I told him I had a trip planned to go with Grace and her soccer team to Spain to watch them train with the coaches from Real Madrid. With trepidation, I asked, "Should I cancel my trip?" He replied emphatically, "No! We will have you ready to go by mid-March." What glorious words to my ears! I would soon be thinking clearly and have the energy to take on an overseas trip with my daughter's soccer team.

The protocol was difficult, but it was well worth it. Dr. Nick was correct. I was regaining my health and was well enough to take that fun excursion overseas with my daughter, Grace. I learned from this entire ordeal to never take my eyes off the prize. When I started fearing versus having faith, I made decisions that could have prolonged our healing process. I learned a great deal from that illness, which I use almost every day for my family and others who are struggling with their health. Pray first, listen for direction from Him, then follow His prompting!

CELEBRATION

TAPESTRY OF GRACE

"Lord, thank you for all the teachers and amazing women You have put into my life who have taught me Your Word, served with me, encouraged me, gently corrected me, and prayed fervently for my family and me. You are amazing, Jesus! Thank You for being my best friend!"

T hank you for taking this journey with me, reading what I've remembered, documented these simple prayers, and reviewing God's amazing answers. God Almighty truly brings things full circle—weaving the perfect tapestry of grace. Let me explain. Remember the story of my simple prayer, *"Lord, should I keep working?"* If not, turn back to Chapter 4 and refresh yourself on the amazing dream I had, where I was flying around the room praising the Lord. After I read that chapter to my hairstylist, Amanda, the Lord was so sweet. He kindly revealed to me who the family was in that dream. It was my beloved friend Patricia Anthony, her husband Dean, and their two beautiful girls, Vanessa, and Emily. I had the joy of leading them to the Lord seven years after that incredible dream. Remember the fireworks story from Chapter 29? In the middle of the night, the friends we called to provide a roof over our heads were the Anthony's. I will never forget the conversation my husband had with our kids. It went something like this. "Kids, God spared us. We are safe, and we will get through this. We are not victims; we are victorious because of Jesus." He was so right! It was in Dean and Patricia's home where Andy spoke those words of truth to encourage our children.

Remember Chapter 30 when the Lord spoke to me, **"You will be well again, but it's going to take time?"** Well, Patricia was one of the friends who helped me get to the hospital, prayed fervently for my healing, coordinated meals for my family, and did so much more. In addition, the Lord gave her a vision and a verse that she so faithfully painted on canvas. I clung to that verse, 2 Kings 20:5, summed up in her painting as, "In three days, you will be well again."

Now, think back to the last story about my family's health crisis and Dr. Jay's book *5 Steps to Restoring Health Protocol*. Patricia was one of the friends who jumped in to help with our middle school girls' small group, which I co-led. She and another friend, Tina McGlynn, took over and led the precious group of girls when I was unable to lead. The process to get well was a long and hard fight because my entire family was ill, except Andy. I panicked and was not grounded in the Lord. I can tell you, without a doubt in my mind, my dear friend Patricia was praying for me to come back to rely entirely on the Lord and to put Him first and foremost in my life. She had written scripture on her chalk wall as a reminder to pray for us. When Andy and I arrived for a small group Bible study, aka home church, at her house, I knew the scripture was a reminder for her to pray for me. That day, when we showed up, she knew she could erase that verse because the God who sees had answered her prayers. Patricia was not the only one praying for my health and my obedience. Many more were praying, who I have cited in this book, including Dr. Dolores Jacoby, Tina McGlynn, Sue Puchferran, and many more I may never know about until I meet them in heaven.

I am encouraged as I ponder the name of this final writing, *Tapestry of Grace*. I am thinking about and thankful for all the women and men in my life who taught me the Word—who taught me how to forgive and how to love. Please understand my heart. This chapter is not about me. It is about what the Lord has done through other godly people. They have blessed me with their prayers and wisdom. I know I have a long way to go, and I am excited to be on this journey. Our lives are not just about ourselves but, more importantly, about others. I must stop and pray a simple prayer of thanksgiving. *"Lord, thank you for all the teachers and amazing women You have put into my life who have taught me Your Word, served with me, encouraged me, gently corrected me, and prayed fervently for my family and me. You are amazing, Jesus! Thank you for being my best friend!"*

If you have not accepted Jesus Christ as your Lord and Savior, what is holding you back? An eternal relationship with God Almighty is but one act of faith away. Do not waste another day of your life. Do not let excuses, past hurts, and lies of the enemy get in the way. Time is short. We cannot get one day back. Join me in living our lives for God's glory. Let's fill up the boat with lifelong learners and doers of His glorious and perfect will. He has big plans for you! Live victoriously, one day at a time. Please do me the honor and pray with me this simple prayer.

"Lord, please forgive me, for I have sinned against You. I am not perfect. I understand You didn't come for perfection, because Your Son is perfect. Thank You for taking my sins and nailing them on that cross. Jesus, You did not deserve death; I do. I trust You, Jesus. You are God's one and only beloved Son. I believe in You. I want to walk with You, get to know You, and love You with all my heart, mind, soul, and strength. I want to love others the way You love me. Thank you for your forgiveness. In Jesus of Nazareth's glorious name, I pray. Amen."

My beloved friend, if you prayed that simple, salvation prayer, angels in heaven are singing a glorious song over you right now. I welcome you with loving arms! If you are not part of a Bible-teaching church, get there now! Start serving, get baptized as a believer, and get busy studying the Word. If you are brand new to the Word or you are coming back to Him after some time, open the Book of John and begin again. I know you will be blessed by the Word for your effort.

FINAL THOUGHTS

Thank you for taking the time to read my God stories. I pray that these narratives have brought you closer to the heart of our Lord. It's so important to recognize the depth of Jesus' love for you, and I encourage you to dive deeper into His Word if you haven't already. I find great value in participating in Bible studies with others, especially women. The Word sharpens us, grounds us, and keeps us on the right path. Together, we can share stories that inspire and uplift, fostering mutual growth in faith.

Years ago, I decided to download the *Thru The Bible Reading (TTBR)* app, a simple yet powerful way to engage with Scripture daily. The app breaks the Bible into manageable morning and evening readings, making it easy to read or listen through the entire Bible in a year. Since I tend to feel worn out by the end of the day, I prefer to tackle both readings during my quiet time in the morning. If you›re ready to dive in, find a time of day that fits your schedule and go for it! There's no pressure—just a helpful suggestion. If daily reading feels overwhelming, consider *My Simple Prayers: All-Inclusive Workbook*—a focused, 31-day Bible study based on the lessons I've learned from my God stories. With a donation to one of my three favorite local ministries, you can download it at *MySimplePrayers.com* or find it through your preferred bookseller.

I encourage you to gather a group of your favorite friends and embark on this six-week study together. Each day of the study offers a Simple Prayer, a Timeless Treasure for meditation, and more. One Timeless Treasure that holds deep meaning for me is a beautiful framed Scripture my dear friend Patricia gave to my mom one Christmas. Although my mom didn't keep it, it now has a place of honor on my dresser. Each morning when I rise, it reminds me to rejoice and embrace the day ahead!

You, too, deserve the love and support of faithful women

as you journey through life. Always remember—you are deeply loved, highly treasured, and never alone.

With grace, peace, and an abundance of love,

Karen

IN MEMORIAM

Before I completed this book, three people near and dear to my heart finished the race. Most recently, Dean Anthony sat up in the hospital bed, and he walked into the loving arms of Jesus. Vickie Schleimer and Pastor Brian Benjamin also left their earthly bodies to be with the Lord. These amazing people are dearly missed here on earth. They walked with the Lord and served Him faithfully. I am one individual who benefited by knowing and having served with them. What a joyful celebration it must have been when these three saints took up their spiritual residence in paradise. I am thankful they lived their lives well. They fought the good fight, finished the race, and kept the faith—what a joy for them to receive the crown of righteousness in eternity (2 Timothy 4:7-8).

ENDORSEMENTS

Karen Langsam is one of the most loving, Godly women that has crossed my path in well over a decade and a half. The book, *My Simple Prayers,* is Karen's oath to God fulfilled. I have been an enlightened witness to her tests of faith, her incredible ability to cling to the grace, faithfulness, and mercy of the Lord and to seeing her be a strong victor in Him, rather than a victim. It personifies Revelation 12:11.

Called to write this book by the Lord, she has been obedient, enduring not only in telling her story and sharing her prayers but by building on scriptural Word and Biblical truth. Like the ocean is made up of millions of drops of water, Karen's simple prayers fill the golden bowls of prayers before God's throne (Revelation 5:8). Those prayers are poured out in loving answers for you, me, and anyone who this saint prays for in His timing!

I believe this book will be a blessing to you and will lead your soul to a stronger walk with God. When I read it, I heard Karen's fun, engaging voice and pure intent pour out onto the pages. This book is for everyone. Be sure to read this book and use its accompanying all-inclusive workbook to strengthen a more loving walk with or return to your Savior. I endorse it fully and pray it goes far and wide. This is all for His glory!

Dr. Dolores Jacoby
Light of Life, John 8:12 Project Center for Healing
Port Townsend, Washington

My Simple Prayers is a beautiful testament to God's elaborate love. Karen shares 31 of her stories of God's constant intervention in her and her family's lives simply because her faith is strong, and her asks are specific. These stories will make you smile, cry, laugh, and, best of all, want to pray. It is a roadmap for building a strong faith, a strong marriage, and a strong family while living our flawed lives. I hope you will enjoy her stories as much as I did.

Zona Trahan
San Antonio, Texas

I have known Karen for nearly 23 years, and I have never met anyone with a bigger heart for Jesus! She is connected to and filled by the Holy Spirit. Her faith is real. Karen is sincere and her purpose is quite clear – to obey God and share the good news. She wrote *My Simple Prayers* because of God's calling on her heart, and He has led her every step of the way, providing the words to say, the people to help, and even the ministries who will benefit. God is using Karen in a mighty way through these astounding stories of simple, heartfelt prayers. As you read, you will see the many ways God responds by healing, protecting, blessing, correcting, and saving. Karen references scripture throughout the *My Simple Prayers - All-Inclusive Workbook* and gives the reader an in-depth study of the Word. You will enjoy this book and be forever changed because of it. It will certainly lead you to a fuller and richer prayer life.

Stacy Howdeshell
Houston, Texas

God has perfect timing! He knows all and operates in a magical way that we can't quite put our finger on, but with review we marvel at HIS goodness, intension, and amazing love.

My Simple Prayers book and the *My Simple Prayers - All-Inclusive Workbook* is truly a gift from God, from Karen's mind and heart put into words. It is unique and wonderfully comprehensive. A personal story and study that anyone can relate to with the Bible offering us our own personal messages as only the Lord intends for us to hear. It is relatable, simple, and encouraging. The daily lessons for 31 days without a doubt enriches one's life and creates the life-changing habit of daily reaching out to God, inevitably bringing one more joy.

The *My Simple Prayers - All-Inclusive Workbook Study* offers blessings to all through the practice of reciting scripture, drawing, and reflection time. It's a "no excuses" study in terms of everything you need to study is included. For example, when it refers to scriptures, the scriptures are provided for you, not just an address. This approach allows for the reader to completely focus on the lesson and allows for a more in-depth study. *My Simple Prayers* is a true blessing to all, including the new and old believer.

Suzi Dillon
Raleigh, North Carolina

My Simple Prayers is simply a joy. While it is timeless, it is also mainstream and modern, a must-read for every generation. The reader is drawn in seamlessly and effortlessly along for the journey. And the journey leads to love. I highly recommend.

Verne Fitzgerald
Lighthouse Point, Florida

My Simple Prayers is a thoughtful, honest book and study. Karen shares her God Stories to show the reader that God is with us and to remind us to keep our eyes open to see Him at work in our everyday lives. May we have the courage to share our own God Stories so that Jesus may be glorified!

Amy Nobile
Vero Beach, Florida

NOTE RESOURCES

Praying the Names of God by Ann Spangler

Mere Christianity by C.S. Lewis

Making Love Last Forever by Gary Smalley

5 Steps to Restoring Health Protocol by Dr. Jay Davidson

Printed in the United States
by Baker & Taylor Publisher Services

Printed in the United States
by Baker & Taylor Publisher Services